P9-CEZ-843

D0015022

STONEHAM COUNCIL ON AGING
136 Elm Street
Stoneham, MA 02180

It's Only Me

It's Only Me

The Ted Williams We Hardly Knew

John Underwood

TRIUMPH
B O O K S

CHICAGO

Library of Congress Control Number: 2005901425

This book is available in quantity at special discounts for your group or organization. For further information, contact:

Triumph Books
601 South LaSalle Street
Suite 500
Chicago, Illinois 60605
(312) 939-3330
Fax (312) 663-3557

Printed in U.S.A.
ISBN-13: 978-1-57243-695-4
ISBN-10: 1-57243-695-6
Design by Patricia Frey
Editorial production by Prologue Publishing Services, LLC

*For Lori, DeeDee, Leslie, John Jr., Caroline,
and Josh, all my children, whose lives were
touched by Ted Williams—and his by them*

Contents

Acknowledgments

A cknowledgments, in the case of so personal a recollection of a friendship, might not seem entirely appropriate, but I wouldn't be comfortable passing up the chance to credit Neil Amdur, one of *The New York Times*' favored editors. To find out why, you'll have to read the book; I wouldn't want to spoil the beginning. And since that gets me in the mood, I am inclined as well to openly appreciate all those years of having as my editors at *Sports Illustrated* such Time Inc. giants as Andre Laguerre, Roy Terrell, Ray Cave, and Gilbert Rogin, who, during those times, not only put up with me but encouraged my entreaties to go here and there and do this and that for publication with the likes of Ted Williams, even when it meant going to the unlikeliest of places halfway around the world. They undoubtedly understood sooner than I why this was a good thing. And, of course, there's now one more to thank, Tom Bast of Triumph Books, who came to me quite unexpectedly, picked up this particular ball, and ran with it.

CHAPTER 1

"It's Only Me"

L OSS IS MEASURED MOST ACCURATELY by the void that it leaves. The breadth of it sometimes catches us unawares. The day after Ted Williams died, Neil Amdur of the *New York Times* called to ask if I'd write "a reminiscence" on my experiences with Ted; he said he wanted it for the Sunday editions. Through Neil's aegis, I had become an irregular contributor to the *Times* over the years and enjoyed the relationship, but on this occasion, on fielding his call, I found myself more boggled than beguiled. To be sure, I could appreciate from long exposure the stratum Williams' reputation had reached, the almost mythic figure he cut as an American icon who transcended sport and moved—or so it seemed—beyond the customary constraints. In that context, I might have even numbered myself among those who weren't sure Ted Williams *could* die.

But in fact, I knew him much differently than that and in much more earthly terms, and in the den at home that serves as my office in Miami, Neil Amdur's call roused me from the refuge I had allowed myself to take from the news. I suddenly realized I had not confronted the void it would leave. I know when our defenses kick in we mortals tend to cope with that final inevitability as superficially as possible; we commiserate and move on ("Joe Smith died last night . . . how sad . . . pass the salt"). It doesn't make us any less human, it's just the way we are. Now, however, alone in the den but tethered to the call, I was struck in the saddest possible way that a part of my life that I had too often taken for granted had been closed off except to memory.

And at that moment, as if by direction, my eyes fixed on a sliver of black wood standing in a corner of the room between elongated items unsuited for the walls (an African ceremonial spear, a jai-alai cesta, etc.). The office exudes an indifference to order that all but blends out the varied memorabilia that serve as decoration, and it had been a very long time since I zeroed in on any of it. But now the black wood focused into shape and I got a chill up my spine that was palpable. It was the baseball bat Ted have given me—how long ago? Twenty-five years?—that I knew he valued greatly because it commemorated, with the dates etched in gold around the barrel, his 18 appearances in Major League All-Star Games.

And then, as if insinuated into one of those Hitchcockian movie scenes (exaggerated by clashing cymbals) where the protagonist suddenly realizes he's in the middle of a discovery, my mind's eye locked onto other sharpened images: a picture of Ted and me talking on the field in Washington when he managed the Senators; cover renderings of two of the three books we had done together for Simon & Schuster; and after the first, *My Turn at Bat*, had made the bestseller lists, a picture of Bing Crosby and Joe Garagiola holding it open and smiling broadly, as if they'd found a portion only they could fathom.

The sum of all that made me realize how much I had come to love the man, even as one might a favored older brother—or perhaps more appropriately in Ted's case, a cherished but wonderfully eccentric uncle.

And without seeing it, but yet seeing it better than ever, the large dark head and sweeping horns of the sable antelope that looms from the wall in the family room, a trophy I had brought down on safari when Ted and I went to Zambia together. And in another part of the house, the handgun he insisted I "borrow" because I didn't have one "for general protective purposes," as he put it, and then refused to take back. And somewhat gloomily, the rods and reels he had pushed on me to facilitate my becoming "more than just another average fisherman," now mostly out of commission and rusting away in the tool shed.

And in the side yard, a boat, too. A 13-foot Gamefisher that he once endorsed for Sears & Roebuck that I *wouldn't* let him give me, but that I'd bought at his suggestion for my oldest son, John, to use, and that my teenager, Josh, had recently put back on active duty. The last time we saw Ted, Josh reminded him of the boat and how much he enjoyed using it to ply the shallower waters around South Florida. Ted said he damn well better be using it, that being "what boats are for," and that he should "let your father drive it occasionally, too, because he probably needs the practice."

And I thought, too, of all those other heirlooms that I had squirreled away without thinking of them as such: the baseballs he had signed and sent unsolicited to my children; the bric-a-brac from the outdoor adventures we shared on three continents; the letter he had written after my attempt at interpreting for *Sports Illustrated* our first stab at fishing together, flattering me for "capturing the real Ted" (a tacit acknowledgment that there were many public Teds that *weren't* real). And the tapes. Oh, my, the tapes. In the den closet, in a crusted cardboard box long ignored, the hours and hours of conversation—candid, stark, joyous, sad, anguished, profane, triumphant, revealing—that we'd recorded over the years, in places hither and yon, in the way of evaluating a unique persona and a life that had fairly bristled with colossal ups and abysmal downs.

And like a forced accounting, the sum of all that made me realize how much I had come to love the man, even as one might a favored older brother—or perhaps more appropriately in Ted's case, a cherished but wonderfully eccentric uncle. And how I had come to understand how misrepresented he had been in so many ways (and how bruisingly accurate in others, even when he couldn't see it himself), and how much I was going to miss him, even though our contacts had been reduced to the occasional in recent years and all but petered out when he moved upstate and got so sick.

I don't pretend, now or at any time, to have been "closer" to Ted Williams than anyone else. Not at all. I'm not sure I'd have wanted to be. I knew him a long time, but others certainly knew him longer. If I numbered myself among his "good friends," I would also concede that he had a lot of those, moving around him like pilot ships in a crowded harbor. But that was always a pretty volatile anchorage; a number of the more obvious ones had eventually dropped out, sometimes traumatically—and sometimes because, quite frankly, Ted Williams didn't always treat friends the way friends ought to be treated. Besides, we were an unlikely pairing. I was, after all, a writer, among a subculture he routinely disparaged, and was relatively late coming into his life, being a generation younger. We traveled mostly in different orbits. But we connected, for reasons I now see as obvious.

We had met years before when he was near the end of his career and I was just beginning mine, on scholarship at the University of Miami and writing for the *Miami Herald*. I was on assignment at a horse show on Dinner Key where he sat alone in a front-row box, and the show's hostess insisted on taking me over to say hello. I was not eager, having heard and read of his active antagonism toward what he called "the knights of the keyboard." But I went anyway, and instead of a rebuff, got an invitation to join him in the box.

We talked for more than hour. He seemed glad to have me drop by. I remember thinking (prematurely, of course), "Gee, what a misunderstood guy." But though surprised by the courtesy, I wasn't overwhelmed. I wasn't a fan. As a kid, in fact, I had harbored an ongoing resentment for the pain he had inflicted on the pitching staffs of my beloved Detroit Tigers. I was a pitcher myself—or at least fancied myself one, having labored without distinction at that position through boyhood—and took it personally. But, I admit, I liked him from the start.

In all those hours of give-and-take, he never once shied away from an issue, never once closed off a topic.

His invitation to tarpon fish for the *Sports Illustrated* story years later led to additional contacts and then a series on his life in *SI*, then the autobiography, then a book on "the science of hitting" (his idea, title and all), then a book on fishing. We enjoyed from the beginning an active partnership, far-ranging to the extreme. Beyond the comic tennis we played with such fierce irreverence and the dogged scouring we did of the waters off our mutually beloved Florida Keys, we fished and hunted in Canada and Arkansas and Middle America and Africa, and walked the streets in far-off places like Nairobi and London and San Jose, Costa Rica, together, sometimes into the wee hours if we were caught in a time zone change, because we both loved to walk. And we talked . . . and talked . . . and talked—at ballparks, in open boats, in duck blinds, in automobiles, on airplanes, in hotel rooms, on the porch overlooking the Miramichi River at his lodge in New Brunswick, in the backyard of his house on the Florida Keys, over bargain meals in the hole-in-the-wall restaurants he favored, delving freely into each other's convictions and passions and doubts and prejudices.

No territory was off limits. We probed the mistakes of baseball and the duplicity of politicians and the frustrations of golf—and the sheer, utter joy of serendipitous sex (his reputation as a ladies' man was well deserved, and held true into his seventies). We talked about people we admired, and people who had disappointed us, and people who had saved us from our mistakes; and we talked about religion and war and his great, abiding love for the Marine Corps, and about Joe DiMaggio and "Shoeless" Joe Jackson and Richard Nixon and John Kennedy and Errol Garner, the jazz pianist, and the ins and outs of cooking chicken.

If I didn't see then what was happening, I should have. We achieved a trust both mutual and implied—and a wavelength free of inhibitions—and when he became comfortable with that, and was gratified by the results, I think we sealed a friendship that was unique to him. Not because of anything special about me, but because he enjoyed being able to confide in someone about the things he'd kept inside, from way back. I believe that because in all those hours of give-and-take, he never once shied away from an issue, never once closed off a topic. More than a few times I was taken aback by how forthcoming he was, often with things I would have thought classified and wasn't sure I wanted to hear. But I think it became a kind of catharsis, allowing him to vent his most harbored frustrations and prejudices about those he loved and those he hated, and about the triumphs and mistakes he'd made, sometimes at the ballpark, sometimes away from it, and sometimes in boardrooms, and sometimes in bedrooms.

The trust, though sorely tested once or twice, never wavered, and the manifestations of it were more than just oral. When he was approached by the owner of the Senators, Bob Short, to become their manager (and thereby break his vow to never, ever do such a foolish thing), he handled much of the negotiating from the den of a previous home of mine in Miami. We made several real estate deals together—ones I brought to the table because they were the ones I could afford. When he decided to risk marriage for the third time, to Dolores Wettach, then pregnant with their son John-Henry, he asked my help in arranging for a liaison in the Caribbean, far removed from probing eyes. I had gotten to know Dolores, a former *Vogue* model, and liked her, and was glad for Ted that he'd found her, but was not surprised when they eventually split and he took up for good with the woman who (as she herself reminded me more than once) had waited for him through two marriages, Louise Kaufman. Of all the many of that sex who tried to "understand" him, Louise came closest—and was the most tolerant when he was at his worst.

And at his worst, peculiarly enough, he was especially insensitive to people exactly like her. But when she died several years before he did, and I called to commiserate, Ted was beside himself. It was the only time I ever heard him cry.

But oh, how I heard him curse. Anyone who spent time with him did. I don't think it hyperbole to say that if he wasn't the most inventive swearer ever, he would have made the top three, with a bent for descriptive adjectives ("syphilitic" was a staple), even though, as I eventually discovered, his vocabulary was plenty good enough without them. It was another of those quirky idiosyncrasies that marked him, like his fetish for clean hands (yours as well as his) before a meal, and being punctual to the extreme, and expecting no less from others. If you were late to dinner at Ted Williams' house, you could not count on him taking it graciously. If you were *really* late, you couldn't count on him being there. By the same token, if he liked you, he didn't want you to leave and pouted openly if you did.

> *I don't think it hyperbole to say that if he wasn't the most inventive swearer ever, he would have made the top three.*

The big items in Williams' life—all those records, the .400 season, his service in two wars, etc., etc.—that mean so much to so many people are, happily, available forever in sanctuaries like Cooperstown and Fenway Park. For me, though, it was the little things that emerged to define him, the things that made him, in the end, so very dear. For one, he was much smarter than people realized, especially those among that legion of detractors who never quite got past the bile. To be sure, as long as I knew him he was sensitive about his education (he barely made it through high school), and if he hadn't cared to expose himself to an extended scrutiny, it was probably because of that. I have heard him say, privately, to people he knew *were* educated, "Boy, I wish I was as smart as you." But whenever he said that I recalled that he could describe in scientific terms how the jet engines worked in the fighter planes he flew in combat in Korea, and exactly why the baseballs that he hit with such frequency curved when pitched properly.

He was always hammering (his word) at himself to improve: reading, inquiring, listening. Once, when we were fishing off Islamorada, he announced he had just bought a set of the World Book Encyclopedia. He said, "I know I'm going to be in those books all the time. Every night I'll be in those books." He was 50 years old.

And who, in the end, was smarter than whom? When Monday morning came around, the company executives and corporate heads who garnered the rare weekend to fish or hunt had to resubmit their noses to the grindstone, while Williams just pointed his to the next deer stand, or duck blind, or fishing hole. He had carved for himself the idyllic, responsibility-free outdoorsman's life he dreamed of from those early, mostly bleak childhood days around San Diego when he hunted jackrabbits with a borrowed rifle and fished the nights away with a home-made pole. He told me several times how much he envied the life Zane Grey led, "traveling the world in that three-masted schooner, fishing where he wanted, living where he damn well pleased, answering to nobody's schedule but his own."

The controlling factor for a man who has "money enough" to do what he wants is the will to resist the time it takes to make more. This, especially, was true in Williams' case, because he never really wanted what "more than enough" buys. He flaunted a lifestyle that "big shots" (his words) could never afford: unpretentious. His buddies during his playing days were the cop on the beat, the clubhouse attendant, the fishing guide, the theater manager—men in whose unthreatening presence he could be as profane as he wanted, and who would put up with his bullying. For luminaries and intellectuals he tended to be gone for the day.

Some of that changed when he was older and thrust more agreeably into the company of "important" people, up to and including presidents, former presidents, and aspiring presidents who happened to be U.S. senators, mostly more interested in being with him than he with them. An avowed conservative, a persuasion we shared, he was a Nixon friend and fan, and endorsed and contributed to George Bush the Father's campaign in 1988, spawning a friendship that led to fishing engagements on the Keys that Ted said were mostly given over to discussions about flying (Bush had been a World War II fighter pilot) and hitting baseballs (Bush had starred for Yale). I once played tennis with Bush in China when he was liaison officer there and remember him making a point, quite out of the blue, to tell me how much he admired Williams.

But Ted was an equal opportunity centerpiece for politicos, when he was in the mood, even though he thought "95 percent of them" were "horseshit" (again, his words). Twice, at my bidding, he consented to informal meetings with Bob Graham, then the governor of Florida and a lifelong Democrat. Another time he included me for dinner at a restaurant near the capitol with Gene McCarthy, the Democratic senator from Minnesota who had cut such an articulate and appealing figure on the Hill (hence the nickname, "Clean Gene"). I was amused by Ted's ability to dominate the conversation, although part of that might have had to do with McCarthy's own admission that he, too, was a "big fan" of Williams.

He had carved for himself the idyllic, responsibility-free outdoorsman's life he dreamed of from those early, mostly bleak childhood days.

But almost no such enticement, political or otherwise, could compromise Ted's lifestyle. He just wouldn't permit it. One of his rejections was a personal request from Robert Redford to serve as an advisor for the motion picture version of *The Natural*. A professed Williamsaphile, Redford borrowed liberally from Ted's autobiography in the movie, including, as the heart of the characterization, his stated ambition to hear people say when he walked down the street, "There goes Roy Hobbs, the greatest there ever was." Ted's biographical version was a tad less grandiose: "There goes Ted Williams, the greatest hitter who ever lived." Hobbs, à la the real-life Williams, also wore No. 9 and batted third in the lineup, and on his very last time at bat knocked the lights out with a home run. (Ted's didn't actually knock out any lights, but, hey, Hollywood has its privileges.)

When he told me about it, Ted said he was flattered that Redford had asked him, and that when he eventually saw the movie he enjoyed it—"a *hell*uva movie, flaws and all"—and sent Redford a note to that effect, but "I was in New Brunswick and the salmon were hot and I couldn't get away."

It was forever such. When he played, he didn't go to cocktail parties, he drank milk shakes and went to bed early. At the art of being a slob, he *was* a natural. The backbone of his wardrobe was a collection of faded Ban-Lon shirts, baggy khaki pants, and rubber-soled shoes. His concession to evening wear was a plaid sports jacket that he pushed into service for all occasions. Ties were not part of "the act," he said. Ties "get in your soup." He didn't go to concerts, he went to John Wayne movies. In later years, when no longer "the Splendid Splinter," he looked a lot like Wayne, and even sounded like him. I told him I thought it was deliberate. He told *me* not to be a smart-ass.

He prided himself on his thrift. I have been with him when he bought socks at the Army-Navy surplus, and the cheapest tennis shoes he could find. One pair curled up at the ends like Aladdin's boots after he played in them awhile. He was oblivious. His automobile of choice for many years was a Ford station wagon (he got a deal), and when his friends came around in Mercedeses, he mocked their logic. Mercedeses were "overpriced." They were "noisy." When hairstyles lengthened, he kept his short, and bragged about cutting it himself.

He said he wanted to live comfortably, not lavishly. At one point, seeking to improve his security needs when Islamorada began listing toward overcrowding, he contracted to buy a house at the posh Ocean Reef Club on Key Largo, but pulled out before ever taking occupancy when he realized he had *rules* to deal with, and a *swimming pool* to mind. After three aborted marriages, he was a man who knew his way around a kitchen, and prided himself in making chicken taste like veal. Veal, he said, was no bargain. When he ate out, it was usually at unpretentious restaurants like Manny & Isa's on the Keys (he knew the proprietors by name, and they put up with his needling) and the Peoples Drug store in Washington. When he treated himself to a "better" restaurant, he made it a point to get there in time for the early-bird specials.

But it was all "part of the act." He chose houses and restaurants based on the comfort they afforded a man in a Ban-Lon shirt, not their societal or resale value, and when he ate early it was not a business decision, it was because he *wanted* to eat early—"bing, bang, boom, get it the hell over with." Until, in advanced adulthood, he began taking drinks harder than malted milk, and expanding his waistline accordingly, he usually made it home in time for the 6:00 news—so that he could get to bed early. To fish early. To do it all again the next day. The routine of a contented man, in a rut of his own choosing.

And the truth was he was not cheap at all—not for the things or the people he cared anything about. He always bought the most expensive hunting and fishing gear, and gave it away by the armload to friends who admired it. When he sensed a need, he could be wondrously generous and charitable. His support of the Jimmy Fund, for children with cancer, is legendary in New England. Roy Curtis, his regular fishing guide on the Miramichi for all those years, and Roy's wife Edna, who served as Ted's housekeeper there, owed their first indoor plumbing to Williams' largesse. He didn't tell me that, they did.

Once, when I was shopping for a house of my own, he came to Miami for one of our tennis dates and asked me to drive him by the one I considered the best prospect. We looked at it from my car, idling in the street, and I said it had everything except a reasonable asking price. "Nice house," he said. "A *helluva* house. What'll it take to make the deal? I'll loan you the difference." I said no, I couldn't do that. He said, "Then I'll *give* you the difference." No again. And he was genuinely miffed by my refusal. For reasons rooted in his past and thereby peculiar to his makeup, I think he considered it a point of honor. I know at restaurants big or small he invariably grabbed the check, no matter how large the party.

> *The truth was he was not cheap at all—not for the things or the people he cared anything about.*

It was over a check that I first saw the dark side of the Ted Williams' moon, and was so repelled by it that I decided to walk away from our relationship before it was much off the ground.

I had heard all the stories about Ted the Social Schizophrenic. How as a player he had thrown bats and tantrums, and busted a water cooler with his bare fist in a fit of rage. How in Boston he had spit and made obscene gestures at the fans when they booed him, and menaced the ever-critical Boston writers with regular harangues. Not acting, he told me later, but *re*acting. "I was mad an awful lot of the time. I think I had reason to be." In

15

other milieus, he threw golf clubs and busted up fishing gear, and cursed and shouted and stormed around. One afternoon, years later, when we were playing tennis in Miami, and he muffed an easy overhead, he threw his racket with such force the handle stuck into the screening, too high up for him to reach. The absurdity of it hit home as he clambered up to get it, and he laughed in spite of himself. I laughed with him, but by then I knew him better, and vice-versa.

I had been forewarned of how bad it could get. We had gotten through that first fishing trip without incident, and when we forged the agreement to spend the time together for the series in *SI*, and word got around the 20th floor of the Time-Life Building, a friend and colleague of mine, Walter Bingham, came to my office to tell me what I was letting myself in for. He described a verbal lashing he'd taken from Williams in a Washington hotel lobby that was "the most demeaning, the most humiliating experience of my life." He said the reason for it still wasn't clear in his mind; the one story he'd written about Ted was practically an encomium. He said he was seeking to do another when he ran into him at the hotel front desk, checking his messages.

He said Williams' tirade began with "Who the fuck do you think you are!?" and went downhill from there. He said he was so shattered by it that he "left the hotel, crossed the street to a little park, sat down on a bench, and broke into tears."

If I'd fully grasped what Walt Bingham had described, or knew then what I learned in time, I might have recognized the signs. We were in Ocala, Florida, where Williams was helping the Red Sox' minor league hitters in the spring, and he came to breakfast in a black mood. No excuse was given, no explanation offered. Conversation—what little there was of it—was taut. His eyes, never large to begin with, seemed to have shrunk, and were perfectly round and unblinking. Even when he wasn't chewing, his mandibles jumped perceptibly.

When we finished eating, I reached for the breakfast check and had it in my hand and was starting to get up when he leaned across the table and yanked it away. "Don't be a big shot!" he said in a voice loud enough to be heard to the four walls. He then unleashed a cataract of epithets that in sheer volume would have satisfied a day's quota for everyone in the restaurant. The words weren't necessarily directed at me; there was nothing really personal in them. But they hit me like a fist.

The anger crowded my throat as I watched him storm out. I sat there for a long time—hurt, stunned, embarrassed. When I finally got up and drove out to the park, I was still seething. When he saw me come through the stands he waved perfunctorily, and went back to work. I waited without responding. Finally, when he was separated from the players, I walked over and told him, as calmly as I could but mincing no words, what I thought of his actions. I stood for a minute, anticipating a response. He said nothing. I turned and left.

At 5:00 I was in my hotel room, packing to leave and framing in my mind what I would tell my editors about aborting the project, when there was a loud knock on the door. I opened it to Williams, looming there with a wry half-smile, his head bent slightly to one side. "Wanta go eat?" he said.

Stunned once more, I nevertheless followed along dutifully. The issue was resolved, without a resolution. In time I came to realize it was the closest he would ever come to an apology. More important, it was the first and only time he ever acted that way toward me, which would make me believe that my drawing the line was not only necessary but pivotal.

Of all the dotty elements of his personality, his tirades were the ones that made the least sense.

I smile now when I think about it, because as I recall, he let me pick up the dinner check.

None of his friends or family ever convinced me they had figured out what made him blow that way. Of all the dotty elements of his personality, his tirades were the ones that made the least sense. It was as if his character had been faultily wired, leaving an endless capacity for shorts, and when one inevitably occurred, all his appeal and charm curdled into something quite the ugly opposite of charming. But who knew when they'd happen, or how deeply they'd cut?

To my knowledge, his attacks, public or otherwise, were never physical, but they might as well have been. I spoke with Walt Bingham again after Ted died, and he could recount, to the last damaged module of pride, everything that happened in that lobby confrontation so many years before. It had been seared into his memory, like a disaster on a battlefield. He blamed it on a "small negative reference" to Ted's fielding that he'd written in the first story, but I disagreed. I don't think it mattered. I think, quite simply, Walt happened along at one of those times and places where the wheels fly off without warning and the vehicle goes over the cliff to a certain flameout.

Did, ultimately, the charm outweigh the churlishness? Of course, it did. But the ominous flip side was never completely banked or blocked from view. The environments he charged or created almost always trembled with tension of one kind or another. The stress factors that forged his personality, going back to that angst-ridden childhood and through his long public period as an athletic phenom who (and this is important because he believed it himself) got no real direction from even the managers of his teams or the owners who paid him for his heroics, was always right there beneath the surface. Even into middle age, he referred to himself as "the Kid" and often acted like one.

The result was that to be around him was to never lack in conversational excitement, often having to do with things *you* said. He was a relentless interrogator if he thought you knew something he didn't, or had said something he knew to be incorrect. He didn't hesitate to dive in. Thus the next charged moment was always a beat away, uninhibited and fascinating to experience. I can still see his silhouette gyrating against the firelight of a tent siding in Zambia, where we had gone after he was named Manager of the Year in 1969. He was lying on his cot late one night remonstrating over the miserable hitting he had seen that year; I was half asleep, not paying much attention. But before long I could hear him grunting softly. I opened my eyes to look and he was on his feet in the tent, swinging away.

In that regard, as long as I knew him, he never tired of expanding on the exponents of hitting baseballs, something he called "the single most difficult thing to do in sport, where you're considered great even when you fail seven out of 10 times." When we did *The Science of Hitting*, he not only agreed to model for the illustrations, suggesting only that the gut that he'd developed be airbrushed out, but recommended that the cover art include a strike zone delineating the precise areas where one would find the "best balls to hit, and the worst." He was forever disdainful of hitters—most especially big league hitters—who didn't know the strike zone. "The dumbest thing a hitter can do. Dumb, dumb, *dumb*."

Remarkably, even as he approached senectitude—but well before the strokes that finally turned him inward—he could still do the things he loved to do and had spent so much time perfecting and enjoying. He could cast 90 feet with a fly rod, right to the nose of a churning Atlantic salmon or a rolling tarpon. He could stand uncomplaining in a duck blind for hours on the coldest day of the year, then in the meagerest of light make a perfect shot. One year when he was pushing 60, the University of Miami baseball coach, Ron Fraser, asked me to ask him if he would throw out the first ball in an NCAA regional tournament at the Miami campus. He agreed, "as long as you go along." But when we arrived at the park—Ted in his Ban-Lon shirt and rubber-soled shoes—Coach Fraser, an unabashed opportunist, upped the ante. He asked if Ted would *hit* the first ball. Again, with some minor grousing, Ted agreed, but made it a point to insist that the pitcher "throw hard."

> *Even into middle age, he referred to himself as "the Kid" and often acted like one.*

The stadium was packed but turned stone silent when Ted settled into the batter's box. A prize sculpture had come to life. The pitcher (Fraser himself) threw him five balls, as hard as he could throw them. Ted hit all five—every one a line drive, dead to right. Two hit the fence. The crowd went wild.

Not all of this came to mind in that brief conversation with Neil Amdur, of course. It couldn't have. But with what portions that did came a melancholy so profound that I wished only to end the conversation and go on to something else. My own form of coping. Besides, I wasn't sure I really wanted to dredge too deeply into the years with Ted. I suppose, deep down, I was nagged by the vague notion that it somehow would be violating a trust.

I told Neil I wouldn't be able to do it, not then. Maybe some other time.

It was on the last syllable that "the Queen" came to the door of the den. In real life, sans royal inferences, she is my wife, and her name is Donna. She had fielded the call originally, and when she appeared I immediately thought, "the Queen," because that had always been Ted's way of referencing her, as in "How's the Queen," or "Tell the Queen hello . . ."

And that, too, stirred memories. Of how much the lexicon of my life had been affected by him, without me thinking it had or wanting it to. Silly little things that he'd say and I'd find myself repeating instinctively. Like when we sat down at one of those low-budget hash houses he frequented and he'd ask the waitress with a straight face, "What time does the band start?" Or when he caught the fish and you didn't: "There's a lot of jealousy in this boat." If more than a little time had elapsed between contacts, he'd phone, and in that unmistakable boom box of a voice, in an affected, self-deprecating tone he knew would translate as sarcastic, he'd say, "It's only me." It became a routine greeting that I have lately found myself imitating: "It's only me."

At the den door, the Queen said, "What did Neil want?"

"He wants me to write a piece about Ted for the Sunday *Times*."

"Do you have the time to do it?"

"It doesn't matter. I told him no."

She was surprised. "Why not? I mean, wouldn't you like to? Wouldn't you think Ted'd want you to?"

"I don't know. Maybe."

"Do it, then. For his sake. For *some*body's sake."

"Let's not get too dramatic about this."

"Well then do it for . . . what was it Ted used to say? 'Just for—'?"

"Yeah," I said. "'Just for fun.'"

She was right, of course. I called Neil Amdur back the next day and did the piece. And when it was in print, I realized there was more to be said, not so much to enhance the big picture of his life, but to illuminate all those little ones that made, for me, the compelling mosaic that was Williams himself. And I remembered something that clinched it: the very last conversation we had had, just weeks before he died. The saddest two minutes I could have ever imagined.

Donna and I were returning to Florida on a car trip and nearing a point on I-75 that put us due east of Ted's home at Citrus Hills, near Hernando. He and Louise, fed up at last with the thickening traffic and declining fishing around Islamorada, had moved there at the bidding of an old New England friend, Sam Tamposi, the Citrus Hills developer. Tamposi had once owned part of the Red Sox. He obliged them with an extravagant (for Ted) home at "9 Fenway Park Drive," in return for letting him capitalize on the Williams name. The last time we'd visited, Ted said to "drop by" whenever we were close enough, and Donna suggested we should at least call.

I did, and reached the nurse who attended him through those final days. She said he was asleep, but that she thought it might be good for him to see friends "to lift his spirits a little," and that we should come on by. I said no, not under the circumstances (a choice I'll regret making the rest of *my* life), but that I'd call again when it was more convenient. She said wait, then, and she'd wake him and see if he was up to talking.

There was a long silence. And then, Ted himself was on the phone.

Except that it was a Ted Williams I scarcely recognized. All the fiber and bristle were gone, as if removed by whatever surgical processes had been used to get him through his various heart repairs. In a voice that was so distant and beaten that it seemed to be coming down a long, bleak corridor, he made a perfunctory greeting and struggled through what was more a litany of pain than a conversation.

I realized there was more to be said, not so much to enhance the big picture of his life, but to illuminate all those little ones that made, for me, the compelling mosaic that was Williams himself.

And when we were finishing, he said something I'll never forget. "John," he said, "if they told me I'd have to live this last year of my life again to be able to keep all the others, I'd say no thanks. Hell no. I'd give it all up not to have to."

When I hung up, I was clammy. I told the Queen what he said. She shook her head.

"What a terrible, terrible waste that would be."

The obvious, of course, is that there was no such waste. The historic Ted Williams very much existed, "flaws and all," and what I contributed to the *Times*, in the way of filling in the blanks where some revelation might have been in order, I have expanded on in the pages that follow. But the reader should be cautioned: this is not a biography. For that you'll have to revert to what has already been written. No shortcuts are provided here.

I can think of a dozen noble-sounding reasons to do this—for Ted's sake, for posterity's, etc., etc.—it being reasonable to believe that the more we know about a Ted Williams the better *we* are, but the fact is I wrote this more to edify than to instruct. To recollect and relive, in manageable form, some of the adventures, and the conversations, and the impressions. Maybe not "just for fun," as a friend of mine used to say, but for a reasonable facsimile.

CHAPTER 2

An Invitation to "Make History"

I F FIRST EXPOSURE TO ANYTHING WORTHWHILE usually sticks as a memory, it is not always with full favor. The first car sometimes turns out a clunker, the first kiss a confusion of lips and noses. My first fishing trip with Ted Williams was one of the most uncomfortably delightful—or delightfully uncomfortable, take your pick—experiences I ever had. I realized in time that I shouldn't have been put off, because to fish or hunt with Williams without being tuned to the degree of his passion for such things, and understanding *him* enough to know when you could afford to relax, was like risking the passage between Scylla and Charybdis in an open boat—doable, but tricky, with almost every waking moment a challenge to the senses. In other words, I came away both exhilarated and exhausted. In fewer words, I loved it. I think.

The catalyst was Edwin Pope, the honored *Miami Herald* columnist who casually suggested at a football game we were attending that I come down and fish for tarpon with Williams. Pope at the time was also serving as a correspondent for *Sports Illustrated*. I was living in New York in that magazine's employ and thus always on the make for writing projects that would take me to Florida in the winter. Pope said he thought he could wheedle an invitation out of Williams, who after retiring from the Red Sox had become more receptive to small invasions of his privacy, even by writers.

Pope made the connection (Williams later said he was softened by the memory of our horse show encounter years before); dates were set, and together with a crack photographer named Charley Trainor, we converged on Islamorada and fished with Ted for three days, almost nonstop.

And I can honestly say now, many trips later, that those first impressions held up. "The Kid," as he referred to himself (not, as some thought, to take the edge off the first person singular, but because Johnny Orlando, the Red Sox clubhouse boy, hung it on him when Ted came to his first spring training in 1938, and he liked it enough, and enjoyed the appositeness of the image enough, to make it stick from then on), brought to it the same hard-eyed intensity, the same unbounded capacity for scientific inquiry he brought to hitting a baseball. To join him in the quest was to be both entertained and educated, as long as you kept reminding yourself that 1) he was a relentless perfectionist, 2) he was better at it than you were, 3) he was a consummate needler, and 4) he was in charge.

The education began at 5:15 in the morning of the first day, when he insisted we get breakfast at his house on the Florida Bay

side of the key because he did not trust us to find our own at that time of the morning. He said he didn't want us to make him late getting started. Like children awakened to strange events, we

> *Ted had been a fisherman almost before he was a ballplayer.*

stumbled into his kitchen to find breakfast well underway: a good two pounds of bacon sizzling on the stove in twin skillets, and the coffee perked and hot. He ordered us to "just sit your asses down and stay out of the road" so that he could finish. "We're making history here. How do you like your eggs?"

Without a quick-enough response, he decided we liked them soft-boiled and brought them to the table hot and still in their shells, then mocked us when we fumbled around trying to get them open without burning our fingers. "Will you look at that?" he said in a loud voice. "Isn't that something?" He fixed a particular scorn on Pope, whose failures must have been spectacular. I couldn't say because I was trying hard to be nonchalant with my own. "*Isn't that something?*" he said. "What an exhibition."

He circled the table and deftly opened our eggs with a knife and spoon that he clicked and clanged together for emphasis. "Boy," he said out of the side of his mouth. "*Boy!*"

One of our guides for the day, a stringy, sun-baked veteran named Jack Brothers, arrived almost simultaneously with a little black cat that had begun mewing at the back door in response to the aroma of Williams' cooking. "Where the hell *you* been, Bush?" said Williams to Brothers. "We're trying to make history and you're sleeping. Pour yourself some coffee."

Brothers said Ted would be pleased to know he had already eaten and was ready to go, but he took a cup anyway. "Bush" was not his name, of course. It is a baseball appellation short for "bush-leaguer," meaning a player who is less than major league, except with Williams it was a mark of accreditation. If he called you "Bush" you were in. He conferred it often on the guides of the area, whom he frequently patronized, even though he did most of his fishing alone in a custom-made, 17½-foot boat. Fishing guides, traditionally, are bullies, but one of the better ones, Jimmy Albright, a Williams regular for three decades, told me they did not bully Ted because Ted knew more about fishing than they did. When he paid them to join him it was mostly for the ride. On this day we were too many for one boat, so he had hired another, younger guide named Billy Grace to meet us at the designated spot.

Breakfast was accomplished at flank speed and included a brief, animated argument between Brothers and Williams involving a statement Brothers made about the schooling habits of a certain shark that inhabited the local waters and had "bit some French guy in the ass." Williams challenged him for a sentence or two, then jumped up and strode out of the room, returning shortly with a large book opened to a page where the shark was pictured. He read a portion of the text that resolved the issue, in his favor.

"Geezus, Williams," Brothers complained, "a guy says something you don't agree with and you pull an encyclopedia on him!"

The little cat was mewing in earnest at the back door as we prepared to leave. "Damn cat," said Williams. "I hate cats. Been trying to run him off for weeks. I've thrown things at him—for crissakes, I've done everything but drown him." He began gathering up the leftover bacon; enough to feed 10 cats. He opened the screen door and fended off the cat gently with his foot. "Get the hell out of the road," he said, and laid the platter of bacon down on the concrete floor of the porte cochere. The cat went to it hungrily. "No sense letting it go to waste," said the Kid.

"All right, let's go," he said. "Let's get serious. It's time to start thinking about fishing. Bear down, Bush. *Let's start bearing down.*"

Islamorada is the jewel inset of a two-mile island called Upper Matecumbe Key, 68 miles south of Miami. Until the word got out about the fishing, it was mostly inhabited by a tribe of big-hearted, hard-headed, industrious white natives called "Conchs," whose ancestors had infiltrated from the Bahamas after first having fled the American Revolution as supporters of the crown. I knew about Conchs. My mother was one, born in Key West, 82 miles farther south. My father was one, too, except laterally. He was born in the Bahamas, and had come to Florida to marry my mother and eventually run his own charterboat fishing business out of Pier Five in Miami. It was a piscine advantage I had on Williams that I pushed as often as I could over the years, but the fact was my father had died when I was four, leaving me with only a vaguely genetic fishing expertise.

As for the Florida Keys and the fishing there, Ted knew both much better than I. He had been a fisherman almost before he was a ballplayer, and had said that when he could no longer hit .300 in the big leagues he would just quit and go fishing. He never proved he could not hit .300 (at 42, in his last season, he batted .316), so he quit and went fishing anyway. Bonefish drew him to the Keys, and the Conchs helped keep him there. The best thing about Conchs, he said, was that they didn't

He gave the impression he could stand there silently and contentedly for hours waiting for the fish, a demonstration of patience he had never exhibited at the ballpark.

make a fuss over him. They took him for granted. He was "Hi, Ted" to them, which meant he could fish in peace, and for that Islamorada was idyllic. The Gulf Stream runs by five miles offshore to the east, a playground for sailfish, marlin, wahoo, and kingfish. Along the coral reefs he could go for snapper, jack, barracuda, and grouper. On the flats of the Gulf side, or Florida Bay: bonefish, snook, permit, redfish, and the champion fighter from prehistoric days, *Tarpon atlanticus*, the silver-king tarpon.

Predictably, Williams soon enough switched to tarpon as his principal quarry, calling it "a big, tough, tackle-busting fish that you catch in what's essentially light-tackle conditions, in relatively shallow water." He was so taken by it, and got so good at catching it, that he eventually inveigled the Islamorada Fishing Guides Association into starting a selective invitational tarpon tournament called the Gold Cup, which he then won several times. The guides said it was the best fishing tournament in the world, and probably the most heavily gambled on.

That first morning we piled into Williams' Ford, and he drove, an adventure in itself. He drove much the way he used to prepare to hit a baseball. Waiting in the on-deck circle or standing at the plate, he was never still. He moved his arms and jerked his shoulders, pumped his bat and squeezed the handle, as if to wring out one more base hit. He drove a car no less convulsively. A highly animated conversationalist, he found it necessary every now and then to take both hands off the wheel to make a point. He then drove with his knees. He did not drive slowly. If you were in the front seat with him, you instinctively adjusted and readjusted your safety belt.

The first day in Brothers' boat was spent mostly east of Long Key, and was punctuated by regular debates over the choice of position, the choice of lures (Williams made his own from dyed bucktail), the reliability of this knot or that. Williams winked at me as he tied one to a favored lure. "Boy, the guides would like to know how to tie *that* knot," he said for Brothers to hear. "That's one knot I'll never show 'em." He said it was a "100 percent knot." Brothers said there was no such thing. They argued about that for a while, too.

To the red Bermuda shorts and faded red polo shirt with the character holes that I came to think of as his home uniform in

Islamorada, he had added a shapeless white hat and slathered an extra layer of protective grease on his lips. He assumed his waiting stance on top of a tackle box, looking out across the water, his left hand on his hip, his right holding a Ted Williams–signature rod and reel made by Sears as part of an endorsement agreement. He said he carefully monitored the manufacturing of that and all other Sears products that bore his name. In turn, Sears put the Williams name only on the top of the line.

There on the tackle box, waiting and watching, sometimes rolling on the sides of his feet, Ted seemed finally at ease, as if the frenetic body language in the car and at the breakfast table had been tranquilized. He made small talk, but it was obvious he did not have to talk at all to enjoy himself. He gave the impression he could stand there silently and contentedly for hours waiting for the fish, a demonstration of patience he had never exhibited at the ballpark. But when the first fish came, his demeanor abruptly changed. He dropped into a slight crouch, like a cornerback anticipating a charge. Where before only his eyes were alert, the prospect of a strike galvanized into action the rest of his body, and when he made his first cast, it was quick and sure.

According to the guides, the average score for tarpon fishermen is one catch for every 10 strikes. Williams averaged one in five. That first day he had four fish on the line, but only one, the third, took the bucktail firm. It exploded into the air, surprisingly close to the boat, and Ted's reaction was instantaneous. He played it, worked it, reeled, kept the pressure on, all the time instructing us, explaining what he was doing, advising Charley

Trainor what lens opening to use and when to shoot, and cautioning Jack Brothers about getting too eager with the gaff when the fish was close enough.

"A medium-size fish," he said, providing a play-by-play. "About 50 to 60 pounds. . . . When he rolls, that's the time to put the pressure on. If you can turn him there, it takes a lot out of him. If he jumps, you get on him again. . . . See how I lighten the drag when it's under the boat? Watch, now, he'll jump. . . . When I say, 'Now,' be ready to shoot. . . . *Now!*" And the tarpon was up again, a shimmering silver obelisk just feet from the boat. But when Brothers reached with the gaff, it slipped the hook and was gone, as if at

> *He said Joe McCarthy was the only real manager he ever played for; that the others were just guys in the dugout.*

that critical moment it had decided the entire episode was a waste of its time, and never mind that it made the Kid look bad.

To that point I had only heard of the carnage when the Williams temper stirred. The fractured golf clubs, the busted bats (and water coolers). Later he told me himself about a similar episode on that same Buchanan Bank when he was going through his paces for a movie photographer there to get footage for Sears and a tarpon he was playing actually jumped into the boat. "I could see by the pattern of its jumps that it was heading right for me, and I kept yelling for him to 'get ready, get ready! Another jump and it'll be right in here with me!' And it happened. A big fish, too, a hundred pounds or more. It was like an explosion in the boat. Tackle flying, blood flying. I finally wrestled it down and was able to take the hook out and release it, and when I asked the photographer if he got it, he said no. He'd stopped to change reels and missed the whole damn thing. I blew up. Paid him off on the spot and told him to get the hell back to shore. Broke my rod over my knee, pulled my anchor up and went home."

If I expected him to treat us to one of those defining "responses" this time, however, I was mistaken. Not that big a deal. He nodded at Brothers. "That's all right," he said calmly. "It happens. It happens."

Meanwhile, I made a few tentative tries myself at getting in the way of a tarpon. Requiring as it does the casting of a heavier mix of tackle within what is still a light-tackle environment, I was careful beforehand not to carry out a fiction that I knew that much about it, and to further insulate myself against potential embarrassment, I pointed out several times that I'd never fished for tarpon at all. Things not done out of habit usually feel awkward, and awkwardness is the mother of error.

I soon enough proved to Ted's satisfaction that if I was no tarpon fisherman, I was also no liar. He took to needling me for what he called my "Chinese casts," and was offering a steady barrage of instruction when, quite unexpectedly, I got a huge, rod-shaking strike. Reflexively from years of fishing, I yanked back to set the hook and felt it catch hold—and was startled twice in rapid-fire succession: when the tarpon jumped, and then when it broke the line and vanished. "Wow," I said.

Williams was paternally comforting. "It wasn't your fault," he said. "It was probably one of Jack's knots." He grinned as Brothers fumbled for words to defend himself, and was still applying the needle when we pulled anchor and went home.

The next day, still without a tarpon, we set up again at Buchanan Bank, and Williams bet $100 against all comers that he'd be the first to catch one—and that he would do so before lunch. He took his position on the tackle box and settled in, and as we waited in the gathering heat, he opened up for discussion a whole series of subjects, sampling each as if it were an unlabeled canned good, offering something to chew on.

There is a difference between knowing and knowing it all. The things Williams knew and felt sure of he was adamant about (baseball, the caliber of a hook, the value of his time); the things he did not know, or had an honest intellectual curiosity about, he *wanted* to know. He wanted to know what you thought, right then, right there in the car, in the living room, in the boat. From Charley he wanted to know about cameras, and demonstrated an impressive knowledge himself by the questions he asked. Listen, Edwin, tell me about Joe Frazier. Is he really that good? Was Shoemaker better than Hartack? Why? What do you think about Vietnam? Do the networks tell it straight? Why did *Sports Illustrated* pick *that* guy for Sportsman of the Year?

Without being asked, he carted out some of his stronger feelings about baseball: how it would better serve a faster generation if the season were limited to 140 games, and how too much leisure time—and too much television—was keeping talented athletes off

37

the diamond, and what a shame that was. He said he still felt baseball took more individual talent than any other sport, more
individual work, more of the kind of ded-

*The only notable
expression of his
singular presence was
the name Williams
in small script on
the front screen door,
and there was little
on display to
associate the name
with baseball.*

ication that you are most likely to get
from loners. He said Joe McCarthy was
the only real manager he ever played
for—that the others were just guys in the
dugout. He said he thought "Shoeless"
Joe Jackson should be in the Hall of Fame
because his role in the Black Sox scandal
was questionable on its face and never
proved. He also said that he would be less
than honest if he expressed surprise at
having been elected to the Hall himself in 1966. "I felt I had the
record for it, but"—familiar wry grin—"I thought a couple of the
knights of the keyboard might try to keep me dangling awhile."

It was just after 11:00 o'clock when the tarpon hit. Actually,
it hit the Kid's second cast; it passed by his first, spooking
slightly, and he had to put the second one out 80 feet, and on
the button. The tarpon jumped, exposing its great body, the
scales jangling like castanets. It was much bigger than the one
Williams had lost the day before. He planted the hook with
three quick tugs on the rod and immediately joined the battle,
moving with the action, knees bent, knees straight, leaning,
standing upright, sitting down, talking, checking the drag,
ordering Jack Brothers to maneuver the boat. Sweat and suntan
oil converged in his eyes, and he swiped at it with his left hand.

We were a quarter of a mile from the spot where the tarpon hit when he got it up to the boat. He then had to frantically pass the rod under the bow and grab it on the other side as the tarpon made one last desperate try at escape.

When its nose thudded into the stern of the boat, Brothers moved to gaff it. "I'll tell you when, Bush," Ted shouted. "I'm going to put him right there at the side. Don't do anything until he's ready." He counseled Charley Trainor, in the other boat, on what was happening, and yelled to Billy Grace to move him in closer. "C'mon up, Billy, damnit, c'mon up!" Jack had the gaff poised. "Don't scare him, don't scare him. *All right* . . ." and the gaff was home. They hoisted the fish into the air and checked the weight gage. "Ninety-five pounds," said Jack Brothers. It had taken 35 minutes.

"A guide's dream," said Brothers. "All you do is pole the boat and gaff the fish when he says gaff it."

They lowered the stricken tarpon into the water, and Brothers began to work it around with Ted's help, washing water through its gills. Gradually it began to revive. "He's going to make it," Ted said, pleased. "He's all right, he'll make it. He'll make it unless some shark comes along and bites his ass.

"All right," he said. "Lunchtime."

The Kid's home in Islamorada was pretty easy to find once you found it the first time.

There were a couple of faded signs, one tacked to a telephone pole, that marked the intersection of Madero and List roads near the house, but they were not to be taken seriously. If you asked a Conch where he lived you would be directed by landmarks instead of streets. The lot was five acres, with the two-story, two-bedroom white stucco house backed up to a small lagoon on the bay side, where Ted had a concrete dock. Coconut trees hung over the water.

The front of the house was camouflaged by a grove of rubber trees, gumbo-limbos, and sea grapes, all tucked in by a chain link fence with a NO TRESPASSING sign for emphasis and a burglar alarm for added protection. Separated from the main house was a small shed where Ted kept his fishing equipment and tools for tinkering and tying lures. All in all, the house fairly reeked of unpretentiousness. If you were trying to sell it, you'd have called it "comfortably functional."

After Ted's death and I don't know how many other owners after he quit the Keys and retreated to Citrus Hills, the house was advertised by an Islamorada real estate agency as the "historic Ted Williams estate" and said to include "beautifully landscaped" property, carports (plural), a "private boat basin," a "circular" dining room, a garden patio, *three* bedrooms, a "lush" master suite, and "incredible views of the sea" (assuming you were willing to accept Florida Bay as the sea). It was offered for sale at $2.25 million. How much of that was tied to the "historic Ted Williams" connection would be hard to say, but either way, my guess would be that the Kid would have been appalled.

For his years there, the only notable expression of his singular presence was the name Williams in small script on the front screen door, and except for the den upstairs, there was little on display to associate the name with baseball. The book of photographs in the living room was mostly of fishing triumphs; there were mounted fish hung variously around and two beautiful Atlantic salmon flies suspended in glass on top of the TV set. On the cyprus-paneled den walls were pictures that went back: a skinny boy-man with curly hair and a handsome smile, standing at the train station in Boston in a double-breasted suit and brown-and-white wingtip shoes, proof that he had once consented to such encumbrances.

He admitted that his infrequent attempts at golf eventually disintegrated into a series of broken club heads and bent shafts.

There were other pictures, too: one autographed by Cardinal Cushing, another of Ted and Casey Stengel at Cooperstown when he was inducted into the Hall of Fame, and one of the Kid in his prime, swinging a bat. But dominating through the house were snapshots of his first daughter (then his only child), Bobby-Jo, tracing her metamorphosis from stringy-cute, when they were fishing buddies, to rounded-winsome, when she made him a grandfather. She was everywhere—under glass on tabletops, on walls, standing partially upright on bureaus. He had wanted a boy.

Years later, when he took the model Dolores Wettach as his third wife, there was a general rearrangement and, as a principal conversation piece, a quite spectacular rendering of Dolores herself in the nude on a wall downstairs. But that first time I was there, the eye-catchers were less sensual: the 1,245-pound marlin he caught in Peru, the 500-pound thresher shark he caught in New Zealand, and his favorite for recollecting, the 20-pound Atlantic salmon he got the day after he beat out teammate Pete Runnels for the American League batting championship on the last day of the 1958 season. The Atlantic salmon was his favorite quarry, and for that one he had to travel all night to make it to the Miramichi before the fishing season closed. The 1958 batting title was his last. He was 40 years old at the time.

Most tellingly, there was an impressive collection of books strewn about the house, but none of his baseball trophies. He said his trophies were "up north." He said he'd "have to get them down here" one day. (He did, but a long time later, when his baseball museum was opened in Hernando and they were needed there.) He said he had become an avid reader, and would not leave a page unturned if it pertained to something he was interested in or found cause to examine. He had accumulated a virtual library of how-to books on golf. He said he preferred Cary Middlecoff's teaching to Ben Hogan's, because Hogan was "too technical." He said that his own practical application of the advice given was "rotten," however. "Geez, I sliced everything, you know? I had no control over my long irons."

He admitted that his infrequent attempts at golf eventually disintegrated into a series of broken club heads and bent shafts. He had a theory about that, too. Like Ty Cobb, he was a natural right-hander who just happened to pick up a bat one day in boyhood and started swinging left-handed. As a result, his real power hand, his right, was always farther away from the ball at contact. He believed this diminished his power and affected direction. He said he thought he would have been an even better hitter had he started off (and remained) right-handed—and that he might have been able to hit a golf ball straight, too. Or at least straighter.

His celebrated penchant for privacy had evidently not been diminished by the years. His phone was unlisted. It was not even printed on the receiver. When it got to be too well known, he changed it. If you wanted to get in touch, it required liaison with his secretary, then *he* called *you*. And when he said he would call at 7:30, he called at 7:30. When he eventually entrusted me with his number, he made it clear I was on probation, much as the fishing guides had been in Islamorada when they were practically the only ones who could reach him without going through channels. The guides, presumably, didn't snitch.

Thus trusting them as he did, they were the ones whose company he sought off the water and away from his house. Often in the mornings at daybreak he materialized at the Islamorada Tackle and Marine store where the guides congregated and hung around, bantering and exchanging tips and hints and partialities. He was especially close to Albright, probably because Jimmy treated him without reverence and gave as good as he got. He was, in fact, visiting the Albright house when word arrived that he had been called back into the service for the Korean War in 1952, and when an AP reporter came around to seek him out, the Kid jumped into one of Albright's closets.

Albright blithely invited the reporter in, and deliberately small-talked for an hour as Williams molted in the closet.

Once or twice a week Ted would forego his own cooking to patronize the small Cuban-style restaurant named Manny & Isa's, just on the other side of the Overseas Highway on the crumbling little road that *used* to be the highway. He preferred it there, because recognition was less likely, he could wear his fishing uniform, and the food was excellent. I got to know Manny and Isa in time. Manny had been the cook at the more fashionable Green Turtle Inn down U.S. 1 before he struck out on his own with the black-eyed Isa, his wife, who had mastered the intricacies of the Key lime pie, among other Conch delicacies, and was Ted's pet. He did not spare her the needle.

He said he thought he would have been an even better hitter had he started off (and remained) right-handed.

"Veal," he said loudly that second time we ate there. Patrons at other tables looked up knowingly. "People tell me there are a lot of restaurants on the Keys selling veal and saying it's turtle steak. This tastes like veal to me, Isa."

"Oh, no, Ted," Isa protested in a Spanish accent, pouting and shaking her finger at him. She ran to the kitchen and returned with a great slab of what was unmistakably turtle. "See? You see?" she said.

"Well, I don't know," said Ted, making the familiar wry face.

"Oh, Ted, you are fooling me," said Isa, jabbing him on the shoulder.

Cuban sandwiches were ordered all around, as recommended by the Kid. "How about a beer?" he said. "A beer's good with Cuban sandwiches." Drinking beer was one of his more recent vices. When he was younger he was a confirmed teetotaler. He still bridled at being downwind of cigarette smoke, and what he considered the inconsideration of cigarette smokers. When Edwin Pope lit up, he reacted as if he'd been slapped. "What are you, a chain smoker?" he said in a loud voice, and made Pope change seats. "*Damn.*"

When Isa returned with the sandwiches, Ted winked and asked, "OK, Isa, we gotta a schedule to keep here. What time does the band start?"

"Oh, Ted, you know we don't have no band," said Isa, and jabbed him again.

We went out again to Buchanan in the afternoon and fished unsuccessfully until dark. Williams brought a radio along and lay back on the deck so he could watch Jack Brothers put me through my paces. "I want to see this," Ted said. "I've *got* to see this." Before long, however, he was up with us, casting, but it turned out to be a wasted effort all around. At dusk we headed in, and it was after 10:00 o'clock before we were back at his house and able to relax into the big, soft, flower-printed chairs in his living room. Ten o'clock was late for the Kid, but sitting there, yawning, his eyes red, he consented to tell of his evolution as a fisherman.

He told it in an absorbing anecdotal style, absently scratching his head and pulling on his hair and working his arms and legs around, his sunglasses dangling audibly from the V of his shirt.

He said it all began back in San Diego with a neighbor named Chick Rotert when he was 11 years old.

"Chick lived next door, and I guess a lot of people thought he was a rummy or something because he used to drink a lot of that 3.2 beer. But as far as I was concerned, he was a great man. He had a couple fingers shot off in World War I, and then he'd been a game warden for awhile, and he used to go fishing around those bass lakes near San Diego. He'd come back with six-, seven-pound bass, nice, you know, nice bass. I was just fascinated as hell. That appealed to me, you know? So, I finally got a rod and reel, a $3.95 Pflueger Akron reel and a Heddon bamboo rod. Just a straight bamboo rod. But I'll tell you one thing"—he gave me a hard look—"I went out and learned how to cast the damn thing before I went fishing with it. I learned how to use it."

Sometimes, he said, he'd practice on the front porch of his family's little house on Utah Street, casting into the yard and sometimes into the street. "I practiced until I knew what I was doing, standing on the porch in the evenings, maybe waiting for my mother to come home to fix dinner, and sometimes that was 9:00 or 10:00 o'clock. She was always out late, working the streets for the Salvation Army. So Chick Rotert took me bass fishing, and I got some bass, not very big, and from there I tried the surf in San Diego. Used to go with a wonderful man, Mr. Cassie, who lived across the street.

"His first name was Les but I never called him anything but 'Mr. Cassie.' I played on a baseball team with his kids, and he was nuts about fishing. But his kids didn't care anything about it, so he'd take me for the company. We'd drive up to Coronado Beach and fish the whole night, 'til 4:00 in the morning, and then drive back. Except mostly I'd fall asleep, and he'd have to make it with nobody to talk to. I musta been lousy company. He had an ulcer, and all he could eat was graham crackers, chocolates, and milk. It must not have been very appetizing, because after I'd finished whatever I had, he'd give me his, then I'd go to sleep.

> *In the end, he said, reflecting, there were still "so many places" he'd like to try.*

"I loved Mr. Cassie, the nicest, dearest man. He gave me a fountain pen when I graduated high school, the only present I got. And when I was signed with the Red Sox and getting ready to go to spring training, he took his vacation and drove me. All the way from San Diego to Sarasota. I promised him then if I ever made the World Series he'd see it, too. And when we won the pennant in '46, I sent tickets for him and his wife, and they came. When he died, I felt as bad as when my own father died."

He said the fishing possibilities expanded to Minnesota when he was shipped there in 1938 by the Red Sox for his second and last season in the minors, and there he made two notable discoveries: Doris Soule, a "little, dark-haired Dorothy Lamour type" who eventually became his first wife, and the thrill of fishing for muskies and walleyes up at Mille Lacs Lake. "Then I read an article in *Field and Stream* about how a 10-pound snook tied tail-to-tail with a 20-pound muskie would drag the muskie all over the lake. I thought, boy, I sure want to catch one of those snook.

"So I came to Florida for snook, which turned out to be everything they said about it. This was when I was in the service in 1942, stationed at Pensacola, instructing in Corsairs at the air station, and a buddy and I saved up our ration stamps to buy enough gas to get us down to the Everglades. The first or second cast I got a 15-pound snook, and it took off like nothing I'd ever had on freshwater equipment. We had a good day, and we were at this fish house at Everglades City, and I said, 'Gee, we caught a lot of fish today,' and the guy at the counter said, 'Bring 'em in, we'll buy 'em.' 'How much do you pay?' 'Eleven cents a pound.' That sounded good to us, so the next day we kept every snook we caught, 110 pounds of snook, which is quite a little haul. And that's the *first* and *last* and *only* time I ever sold fish."

He said after the service he made up his mind he'd come to Florida a week early just to fish before spring training. "Then a week wasn't even close to being enough time, so the next year I came a month early, then two months, and before I knew it I was a resident of Florida." He said around 1950 he answered the call to try for bonefish on the Keys, "I'd been hearing a lot about bonefish," and that first winter at Islamorada, he caught 67, and "before long I bought myself a house and I was permanent."

He said he should have been more excited about the house "because it was the first I ever owned, but I was *more* excited about the fishing. I wanted to fish every goddamn day, and I did." He said he was sure his love for fishing "cost me an awful lot in life, made me miss out on a lot. That's true of a lot of guys whose drive was slowed up by going fishing, or going hunting, or [pursuing] some hobby."

And in the end, he said, reflecting, there were still "so many places" he'd like to try. He said he'd like to have a big boat he could outfit "and hire a crew and just fish around. I can't think of anyone who had more fun than Zane Grey with his big boat. What a hell of a life he had, you know?"

The next week, with Jimmy Albright as his guide, the Kid won the Gold Cup tarpon tournament for the second time, moving up from 11th to 1st place on the last day when he caught five tarpon in the afternoon. Before the tournament, the betting got lively, and the two of them, Jimmy and the Kid, wound up with $1,100 riding on the outcome. When the bets were collected, he gave the entire $1,100 to Albright, plus an extra $200 he *claimed* he won, but Jimmy doubted. He also gave Jimmy the gold tiepin with the leaping tarpon that went to the winner. The Kid said he did not wear ties. He said he had a couple of clip-ons he called "phony-baloney ties," but they stayed in the drawer.

Albright compared Williams' generosity with the time in 1946 when the Kid, after playing in his only World Series, gave his entire Series check to the Boston clubhouse boy, Johnny Orlando.

Later, Jimmy told me that every morning before they went out during the week of the tournament, Ted stopped at his back door to feed the little black cat. "The cat was so darned determined," said Albright. "He just kept hanging in there, hanging in there. And Ted hates cats, you know."

CHAPTER 3

Telling It His Way

ESS THAN A WEEK AFTER THE FISHING STORY appeared in *Sports Illustrated*, a mailing identified on the envelope only as "Lakeville Baseball Camp, Inc." arrived at my office at the Time-Life Building in New York. Inside, to my surprise, was a one-page letter from Ted Williams, reminding me, pointedly, that it was "not very often" that he wrote letters, but that he thought I'd done "a hell of a good" job recounting our adventure in Florida. (I rechecked the signature to make sure I'd read it right.) It went on: "I have to give you credit, old boy . . . I'm getting numerous letters and calls from friends who know me as I really am and who really got a kick out of the article. It was a great three days, and a great article. Sincerely, Ted."

Journalists who spend much time—*any* time—agonizing over how a subject might respond to being examined in print should not be in journalism, and I say that with the certain knowledge of having spent a lot more time in the writing dodge than I ever intended. Communication in such instances too often begins with "Dear Idiot . . ." and unravels from there. The ones that gush with praise (or appreciation), on the other hand, might make you feel gratified (or exonerated) for a while, but then leave you wondering if you overlooked something.

It was left for a colleague at Time Inc., Jack Olsen, to put this one in perspective. Olsen was an early hero of mine, one of the two best writers on the *SI* staff, along with Gil Rogin, when I went there out of Miami. Like me, he had been tempted in from another realm—in his case, *Time* magazine some time before; in mine, the city desk at the *Miami Herald*—because of the reputation *SI* had gained, at Henry Luce's and Hedley Donovan's prodding, as a writers' magazine. *SI*'s managing editor was another Time Inc. giant, the former Paris bureau chief, Andre Laguerre. Olsen was Laguerre's pet.

On this day, a Sunday afternoon during the week's issue closings, Jack and I were in one of the lesser-traveled halls on the 20th floor playing catch with a scarred-up baseball. He used a spongy catcher's mitt that he said he needed because I was "the only guy on the floor who could throw a curve in the hallway," an exaggeration I never discouraged. (Jack mistook "spin" for "curve." If anything, what I threw was a flaccid version of a slider.) Laguerre let Olsen get away with such things, and Olsen, in turn, rung in various other idlers for a variety of "athletics" during down time (the nok-hockey and wiffleball games were loud and furious), and I didn't have to be asked twice.

We were between pitches when Jack told me how much he liked the Williams piece, so I mentioned the letter. He held up his free hand and whistled. "Hey, man, Ted Williams doesn't send letters to writers, he lobs hand grenades." He asked if he could see it, and I let him. He whistled again. "Save it," he said, grinning. "Nobody'll believe it without the evidence."

> *So many of the things that he ran to were explained by the things he ran from.*

It turned out Jack Olsen knew a lot more about Williams than I did. Jack was a self-inflicted "baseball nut" himself, and a tireless scrivener who even while carrying a full load for the magazine turned out books in such rapid succession that you wondered how he found time to *read* them, much less write them. He eventually finished 27, and as further demonstration of how smart he was, married an *SI* cover girl from one of the swimsuit issues and moved to the far Northwest. He said I should know, since I obviously didn't, that Williams, while always a hot topic, was still mostly an enigma; that entire books had been written about him but always from afar and with no intimacy or revelation because Ted never let anybody get that close. He said he'd like to write one himself, but without hope of direct access, hadn't pursued it. He said I should. I laughed him off. "I'm serious," he said. I laughed again, and threw him another ersatz curve, which he dropped ingloriously.

But a few days later I got called in by Andre Laguerre with essentially the same proposal. I have no doubt Olsen put him up to it, but the interest was genuine. Laguerre said a series on Williams' life, done in first-person (i.e., Ted's words), would be "terrific" for the magazine, since it had never attempted anything like that with a sports celebrity—and because Williams was Williams.

I said I'd make a pass at it. What I *didn't* say was that I wasn't crazy about the idea. As much as I enjoyed recounting the fishing adventure, I wasn't sure I wanted to submit myself to an extended exposure to all that electricity. But I also figured Ted would say no, given his track record, and if I asked and he declined, I'd be off the hook.

But Ted didn't say no. He said yes, eventually. I put a call in to his longtime secretary and confidante, Stacie Gerow, and within hours got a call back from Ted. I told him what the magazine had in mind, and he said, well, he'd been approached to do the same "about a thousand times" and had always declined. But maybe, now, he might reconsider. "How much time would you need?"

"As much as it takes." (If I was going to get a commitment, it had to be total.)

"Good answer," he said. "Helluvan answer." Short pause. "OK, OK, let's do it. I'll get back to you."

He didn't, of course. Not right away. Once he'd closed up at his boys baseball camp in Lakeville, his fishing schedule took precedence and I didn't hear back. So when my own schedule crowded up, making the prospect appear to be fading, I called again. He immediately called back, and just like that we were on, with him setting the times and places. I did the research I needed in order to ask reasonably intelligent questions, and we met in Ocala, Florida. Spring training was starting and Ted was there under contract to help the young Red Sox hitters.

And we picked up, conversationally, almost exactly where we left off on the fishing trip. On benches at the ballpark, at poolside at the motel, at breakfast, lunch, or dinner, and whenever and wherever an opportunity presented itself, we talked, almost always for the record, setting a pattern for open-ended communication that would play out for decades afterward.

And from the beginning I was amazed by his willingness to examine not only the evolution of his talent and achievements, but also to at least try to fathom his sometimes quirky, often radical behavior as a professional: the fits and feuds and emotional binges that marked him then (and mark him still) as one of the most controversial and, ultimately, most unforgettable of America's heroes. For me, a non-fan, it was especially revealing because through this candor he helped me understand actions that had actually prejudiced me against him, or at least against the images I had formed from the things I'd read. So much of the negatives turned out to be inexorably linked to the positives. So many of the things that he ran *to* were explained by the things he ran *from*.

And as the days and weeks went by, I realized something else: that he was venting. That he had become comfortable enough in opening up to those dark corners of his life to risk getting things off his chest, and was now almost eager to do so. But sometimes it took *me* a long time—years on some subjects—to put it all together.

At the beginning in Ocala, he talked positively about how "fortunate" he was to have grown up in San Diego, "where it's always warm and the baseball season was however long we wanted to make it." He spoke of the North Park playground a block and a half from his house as if it were Valhalla, where the field had lights and "we could play until 9:00 at night if we wanted to. I was there all the time. Play, play, play. Horseshoes, handball, everything except basketball, because the ball always seemed four sizes too big." He said he even tried tennis, but he broke the strings on the used racquet somebody gave him "and it cost 15 cents to replace them, and my mother said, 'You better find another sport.'"

He talked about hurrying to fix his own breakfast growing up, drinking a "ton of orange juice" because it was cheap, and expediting everything so he could be at school when the janitor opened the doors "and I could get into the closets and get the balls and bats and be ready for the other kids." That way, he said, he was always "first up" in their pick-up games before class started. Then at lunchtime he'd run home for "a sack full of cold, fried potatoes, and run back so I could get in another 15 minutes of ball before school took in again." He said to make himself stronger, because "I was skinny and kinda weak," he'd drink milk shakes whenever he could afford them. Milk shakes were his conditioner. But availability to ballfields was his making, he said. "I mean, with that and the fishing, I can't imagine having more opportunities to do the things I loved to do."

Besides Chick Rotert next door and Mr. Cassie across the street, his fishing patrons, he went on at length about the playground director, Rod Luscomb, "my first real hero." How he trailed after Luscomb "like a puppy dog for six or seven years," and how Luscomb was always there for him, coaching him, playing one-on-one games with him "when everybody else had gone home for the day." And then how Wos Caldwell, his high school coach at Hoover High, was "always encouraging me, always after me to run faster, which was not easy for me, a tall, gangly kid. He'd start me at home plate, let me get halfway to first base, then come after me with a switch. Usually he caught me between first and second and was hacking my ass the rest of the way." Williams said, with feeling, "I loved Wos Caldwell."

But there was something missing. Something obvious. And, yes, more revelatory now, with the passing of time and his own passing, than when we talked about it then. For all those familiar circumstances you would have expected to hear references to his father, there were none. Not one. No shared fishing trips. No hunting. No playing "catch." No man-to-boy talks. No plaudits or admonitions. Virtually no interaction at all.

Not that he sugar-coated it. To the contrary. He described Sam Williams as a slightly built, straight-haired man—"I got my curly hair from my mother's side"—who "never said much, always very quiet, never smiled," and who was conspicuous mainly for his absences. He said his father "ran a little photo shop downtown where he took passport pictures and sailors from the navy base with their girls, and he wouldn't get home until 9:00, 10:00, so I didn't see much of him growing up." The one thing he remembered clearly, he said, was his father's pride in having run off to join the Army as a teenager and serving in the Philippines during the Spanish-American War (Ted had a picture of Sam Williams on a horse, in dress uniform), and that after military service he'd been a U.S. Marshal in San Diego, "the best job he ever had, his biggest claim to fame."

He said, "I loved my dad, it's not that I didn't love him. But we were never close." When asked how much this might have affected him, Ted brushed it off. He said it was "just how it was, that's all." A way of life. He said his father rarely saw him play growing up, and never when he went to the big leagues. It was Les Cassie, not Sam Williams, who drove him to Florida for his first spring training with the Red Sox.

How much of that reverberated through his own admissions that he "never had anybody telling me what I should or shouldn't have done" when the wheels flew off in Boston would be hard to say. At the time I didn't press him on it, and saw no reason to. Boys grow up all the time without the significant input of fathers and don't always swerve into behavioral problems (as Williams correctly pointed out about my own life when told that *my* father died when I was four). It was as if he had dismissed it as a factor a long time ago, so why dwell on it?

But there was a very significant second half of this erratic equation, the mother Ted "loved so much," but for whom, in the end, he seemed to—no, not seemed to, did *openly*—harbor the greater resentment. He talked about her frequently in those first conversations, mostly in appreciative terms, to be sure, but with a palpable discomfort, too, because she clearly dominated his life in the formative years, and there was much in that domination to be uncomfortable about.

He wasn't just a boy coming into the big leagues, he was a boy impaired by a failed familial base, totally unprepared for the scrutiny (and the criticism). He needed guidance and boundaries. He got neither.

Mae Venzer Williams was half Mexican, half French, and to son Ted's intense dismay, "all Salvation Army." She had joined the corps as a child in 1904, and was affectionately known as "Salvation Mae" and "the Angel of Tijuana" for her work in the seamiest sections of San Diego and across the Mexican border into Tijuana. She ministered "even into the red-light districts" and set records for selling *War Cry*, the Army's magazine. But what Ted remembered most was that she wasn't there for him.

"My younger brother Danny and I would be out on the porch past 10:00 o'clock almost every night, waiting for one of them to come home. I mean when I was eight and he was six, we'd be out there. We didn't know to be 'deprived,' we only knew we were hungry and we hadn't had any dinner, and that my mother was out in the damn street somewhere. Later on, when I was into my teens, she had me out there, too, with the Salvation Army band, and oh, how I hated that. I never wore a uniform or anything, but I was right at that age when a kid, especially a gawky, introverted kid like me, starts worrying about what other kids might think, and I was just so ashamed."

When the Yankees offered him $200 a month to play full-time on one of their farm teams, Mae Williams wouldn't allow it.

He made it clear that it wasn't the Salvation Army he resented, it was his mother's obsession with it. And the degree to which it deprived him of her. "Today I'd be proud to walk with those people," he said, "because they're truly dedicated, but then I'd stand behind the bass drum, trying to hide so none of my friends would see me. And she made me go so damn much. I *hated* it."

He said that when they wrote about his dad years later they routinely depicted him as a "wanderer" and a "deserter of the family," but "that was bullshit. He stuck it out with my mother for 20 years, and finally packed up, and I'd probably have done the same." He said what he remembered most about his parents' marital relations was her complaints about Sam Williams' pipe smoking and his lapses into "beer and wine." She was on him all the time about those things. "My mother was a wonderful woman in many ways, but gee, I wouldn't have wanted to be married to a woman like that. Always gone. The house dirty all the time. Even now I can't stand a dirty house."

He said people who knew him then would have seen him as a brash kid, "and I probably popped off a lot, but I always held so much inside. I never went out with girls, never had any dates, not until I was much more mature looking. A girl looked at me twice, I'd run the other way. You see pictures of me as a kid—*gaunt*. Nervous. Gee, I bit the hell out of my nails, right down to the quick. Even later, when I first started signing autographs, I'd hold my head down."

He said the boys in his neighborhood were "mostly a pretty rough bunch, older guys who drank beer and at least talked about going to Tijuana for women. Things like that scared me to death. I never drank. I never smoked. I was embarrassed about my home, embarrassed that I never had quite as good clothes as some of the kids, embarrassed that my mother was out in the middle of the damn street all the time. Until the day she died she did that, and it always embarrassed me, and God knows I respected her and loved her."

He said Mae Williams' pious influence intruded on his earliest opportunities to capitalize on his baseball. He spoke of that matter-of-factly, too, without rancor, and even saw the humor in it. His first "offer" while he was still at Hoover High and batting almost .500 over his last two seasons was for $5 each Sunday to play for the Texas Liquor House semipro team. "Five dollars was a lot of money in those days, and I was excited. But when I told my mother about it, she said, 'Who'll you play for?' 'Uh, the Texas Liquor House.' If I'd said 'Murder, Incorporated,' I wouldn't have been turned down any quicker."

When, after graduation, the Yankees offered him $200 a month to play full-time on one of their farm teams, Mae Williams wouldn't allow it. She wanted him home. He signed, instead, with

61

the San Diego Padres to play in the Pacific Coast League (for $150 a month) for the last half of the 1936 season and through 1937. That winter, the Red Sox bought him, but he remembered the signing more for the angst than the attainment.

The general manager of the Sox, Eddie Collins, came to the house, "and the only decent chair we had was an old mohair thing that had a big hole you could see the springs through." He said he covered the hole with a five-cent towel, "and that's where Collins sat, and from where I was I could see a mouse running back and forth along the baseboard." His mother did the negotiating, he said, while his father puffed his pipe in silence, and the result was a two-year contract: $3,000 for the first, $4,500 for the second, and a $1,000 bonus for the parents. Mae had bargained herself into the mix, and Ted accepted that as her due. From that point on he grew as her benefactor until he was the sole provider during and after World War II, and until she died. The only thing that he resented about it was his brother Danny, a practicing ne'er-do-well, "always coming around trying to con her out of it."

When he recounted those years, Ted said he never missed them. To the contrary. That while the boy in him relished his first experiences as a professional—the train trips into Seattle and Portland, "seeing the natural beauty of the Northwest," signing for his meals ("we were allowed $2.50 a day, and I ate everything in sight")—he said he was "glad all that was over. I mean, I wouldn't go back to being 18 or 19 years old, knowing what was in store, the sourness and the bitterness. Knowing how

I thought the weight of the damn world was always on my shoulders, grinding on me. I wouldn't go back to that for anything. I wouldn't *want* to go back."

After the Red Sox sent him to Minneapolis for his last season in the minor leagues, he never returned to San Diego to live. He said, "Home was not a happy place to me."

Now, step back for a minute and see this in the totality of Ted Williams' life. On the front side, an unhappy home, and a mother (and father) he loved but could not count on. Note within that context how often he used the word "love," a concession to feelings that critics writing about him in Boston would have made you doubt he had, or would even admit to having. And perhaps more telling, "loved, but——." The consequences of all that doubt and distrust.

And on the back side, a continent removed from his upbringing, the bitterness wrought by the career-long tensions and conflicts with—and antipathy for—the two modifiers that can do the most to damage a professional athlete's peace of mind: the writers in the press box and the fans in the stands. He wasn't just a boy (19 but still very much a teenager) coming into the big leagues, he was a boy impaired by a failed familial base, totally unprepared for the scrutiny (and the criticism). He needed guidance and boundaries. He got neither. His "father figures" in the Red Sox management, men that he truly cared for, owner Tom Yawkey and manager Joe Cronin, mostly took a pass. Ted said as much himself, repeatedly. That the Red Sox deserved part of the blame for all those years of rancor, "especially when I was a young player and should have had some protection to head these things off before they got worse, which they always did."

To be sure, any armchair psychologist worth his presumptions could argue that such is often the case with the achiever. That these profound negatives in his life could be seen as having helped goad Williams into greatness—the irritants inside the oyster that spin into the pearl. After all, isn't that what it's about? Success? Achievement? Marketable notoriety? Williams certainly could have subscribed to that, given the results. But by his own admission, he was never, *ever* happy with the world around that pearl of a career. Or about much of anything else beyond his brilliance within the chalklines of the ballfield, and the solitary things—the fishing, the hunting—that he ran to, to escape the ache. Now, when he's gone, I find that especially sad.

But to take it an item at a time. How much did that woeful family background, and his ongoing feelings of alienation in Boston, affect his own blown attempts at family with the years? There is no way of knowing for sure, but he was married three times, and divorced three times. And he wound up, unmarried, with the one woman who, by her own admission, "could put up with him," Louise Kaufman. I knew Louise, and liked her a lot. And witnessed some of what she put up with. I also knew Ted's third wife, Dolores Wettach, and liked her a lot, too. I thought she'd have been perfect for him: beautiful, smart, tough, attuned to the outdoors (she looked as good in jeans as she did in an orange chiffon dress), and she gave him the boy he said he always wanted, and another girl to go with his firstborn from the first marriage. But that didn't last, either.

And I recalled when they divorced that he had asked me before they were married to help get him a lawyer (I did) "to write up a prenuptial agreement." An admission of distrust, built in.

But stay with me for another minute here, with the subject of Mae Williams' influence, and what amounted to the chronic dysfunction with women that followed. Keep in mind the fact that all this began in his most impressionable years. And that while he was still so

> *At the very end of his life, who was there for him? Not fishing buddies. Not baseball buddies. Not friends from past or present. Family.*

young and immature (except as an athlete, of course, which often creates false cover), something else happened that most certainly affected him. I know it made a deep impression because when he told me about it 30 years after the fact he could recall every detail: the setting, the circumstance, the play-by-play. I passed over it when I wrote the series on his life, thinking it poignant enough but irrelevant, and when the series became a book, I saw no reason to stick it in, though Williams never indicated it was off limits. But now, for the subject at hand, it needs to be recalled.

It was, he said, his first sexual "encounter," and it happened in Detroit, on a road trip, during his first season (1939) with the Red Sox. At that stage of his life he was not even close to being comfortable with girls. He said he saw himself through puberty as skinny, gawky, and shy, and so introverted that he had had "only one date in high school," and the one was no fun at all. The episode in question happened during the awkward, experi-mental period when he was evolving sexually, and he described it as a near disaster.

He became, as a young man, an ongoing draw for women's attentions (and intimate affections), but he suffered through those three aborted marriages and a series of uncomfortable romances.

A young woman "about three years older than me" had pursued him at the ballpark, and then at the hotel where the team stayed. After several phone calls, he agreed to meet her for a movie. Beyond that, he was wary. "I was scared of those things then," he said, of how "sex could screw up my career if I got gonorrhea," which he was told was ever-threatening "and a son of a bitch to get rid of." So when the young woman followed up with a visit to the hotel, he "got a kid to go to the drug store for some pro-phylactics," and let her come to his room. He said he was so naïve he had to be shown what to do ("I'd never had sex before") and that when it was over, he felt "degraded."

"I said, 'Geez, I'm never going to do that again until I get married.' That's the way I felt."

In the off-season, he got to liking an ex-cheerleader he had met in high school and put the Detroit misadventure behind him. But when the Red Sox returned to Detroit the following season, the woman called and left messages at his hotel. He ignored them. Then, on the last day there, "I get in late, about 11:30, and Charlie Wagner was my roommate . . . and I get a two-page telegram where she's gone away and had my baby. Well, for crissakes, you talk about an emotionally upset guy. . . . And I went to bed and started to cry, and [Wagner] heard me and I told him about it, and showed him the telegram. Charlie was about five years older than me, and he'd been around."

He said Wagner calmed him down and told him "not to worry," and got him to take the "problem" to Joe Cronin. "And this is one of the things that endeared me to Cronin." When given the whole story, Cronin brought in the cops, "and come to find out this gal had tried to get [Hank] Greenberg [the Tigers' star player] in trouble, too. And that was the end of that." But he said it without conviction, as though the images were still fresh in his mind.

How much such a trauma might have affected Ted Williams' feelings about commitment generally and women in particular is impossible to say, of course. But considering all the truncated relationships that followed, you'd have to conclude that it must have played in. He became, as a young man, Hollywood handsome, "star quality," my wife Donna called it, an ongoing draw for women's attentions (and intimate affections), but he suffered through those three aborted marriages and a series of uncomfortable romances, and seemed to have concluded that the only place he could coexist was in bed. He once asked me, quite out of the blue, how many women I'd "had," as if it were something you kept score on. And I think he did exactly that. Kept score. But I think it was also evident that he wanted more than that, because he kept trying to make marriage work.

Even if it was a mixed blessing, his son's return to his life was still, well, a blessing.

How hard did he try? Not hard enough. Not from what you saw close-up, which was Ted on edge a lot (demanding too much, expecting too much), and lapsing into spasms of criticism and complaint that sometimes crossed the line into cruelty. None of his wives were spared. His first, Doris Soule, retreated into alcohol after bearing him a daughter, Bobby-Jo, and hanging on for a long time. His second, Lee Howard, a model, got out quickly. Dolores, the third, was much tougher, a high fashion model herself who knew the limelight—she'd been on the cover of *Vogue*—and gave as good as she got. Their scorched-air encounters were famous on the Florida Keys.

Dolores' image is etched forever in my mind from two encounters: the first in New York, when Ted suggested I take her to dinner (he was holed up on the Keys), and I arrived at her apartment to be greeted by a vision in spiked heels and that orange chiffon dress. To fall back on the cliché, she looked like a million dollars—and she was six months pregnant with John-Henry at the time. The second came months later, when I arrived an hour late for dinner at Williams' home in Islamorada.

I don't remember what detained me, but I knew I had made a mistake, and that Dolores would probably pay. Never late himself, Williams hated it when *you* were. He rightfully considered it an affront, and if you were guilty it usually meant an evening of sarcasm and exposed nerve endings. For a man who seemed so insensitive, he was almost pathologically touchy about being slighted. Once, in Africa on safari, when I told him I had to leave earlier than planned, he barely spoke to me for two days.

When I called out from the screen door in front of the house and got no answer, I walked on in and to the kitchen—and found Dolores on her knees, with her head in the oven. The absolute worst crossed my mind.

"Dolores!" I shouted.

She withdrew her head from the oven—to reveal a mass of curlers protruding variously from her hair. She smiled. "Hair dryer's broke," she said. Then, seeing the look on my face and realizing what I might be thinking, she laughed, the big, hearty stevedore's laugh that Ted admired. "It's electric, not gas," she said. "But boy, is Teddy Ballgame mad at you!" Tired of waiting, Williams had gone fishing.

Again, to my knowledge, his abuse was never physical. The adult Ted Williams never struck anybody in anger, male *or* female. He seemed to know better. And to sense, in a peculiarly detached way, that his numbing, belittling verbal intimidation of others was no more than a bad reflection on himself. For a man to whom the fates had been so generous, such behavior in itself was an obscenity, and he had no illusions that most of the damage done was to himself.

Certainly his image was not spared. The perception that became the reputation was that he cared only about himself, and his own gratification. That he was, in toto, a poor husband and a worse father. That his ventures into the boondocks were proof positive that he preferred those things to family life. He was, after all, off fishing in Florida when his first child, Bobby-Jo, was born ("prematurely," as he reminded me again and again). He was lambasted in the Boston press for that. Moreover, he was unrepentant about such things, which always made it worse. He never apologized. One of his Boston critics, as if to summarize his life, wrote, "You are not a nice man, Mr. Williams."

But the evidence I was privy to leads me to believe otherwise. I think in time he regretted those things deeply, and would have welcomed a more inclusive lifestyle. I say that having witnessed more than a few times his pleasure at being with *other* families, mine included. I got the feeling he was envious.

He never once turned down an invitation to dinner at my house, even though it meant driving more than a hundred miles round-trip to get there. He was always solicitous and gracious and respectful of Donna, "the Queen," and though he took charge at barbecues, he was quick to compliment her earliest, comic attempts at elaborate meals. When the chicken arrived on his plate burned black, he said, "That's all right, I like it well done." His interest in my children was genuine, and when time had passed between phone calls, he'd demand answers as to their well being: "How's Lori doing? Yes, and how's DeeDee? What about Leslie? How's John?"

The last time we saw him, when he was slowed by the strokes and all but confined to his Hernando home, he spent more time talking with my last two, Caroline and Josh—about their college aspirations, about their athletics, about Josh's interest in the military—than he did Donna and me. "What a specimen he is," Williams said of Josh, admiringly. "Isn't she beautiful? Isn't she smart?" he said of Caroline. (I have a picture of her bouncing on his knee when she was two, being taught by a Hall of Famer the basics of patty-cake). On this day he had served us a big lunch, with the helping hand of his resident cook, and when it was over and we made the customary moves to leave, he kept finding new subjects to talk about, new things to show us. At one point, Caroline tugged me on the sleeve and whispered, *"He doesn't want us to go!"*

> *You read [the Boston press'] comments now, against the historical evidence of his contributions to the game, and you have to call it nothing less than character assassination.*

And at the very end of his life, who was there for him? Not fishing buddies. Not baseball buddies. Not friends from past or present. Family. His one son, John-Henry.

Much was written at the time about the stains in that relationship, and how the boy he had left behind after that last marriage had come back into his life as an adult to exploit it. How John-Henry, named expressly by Ted after "the railroad man," was always on track for ways to capitalize on the Williams name, and how he'd systematically isolated Ted from many of

71

his longtime friends. All those things appeared to be true. Bob Franzoni, a close friend and benefactor from Vermont, died "disillusioned," his wife Janet told me, that he could no longer get through to Ted. Franzoni had called me once, outraged, when he found John-Henry practicing Ted's signature in the basement of the fishing lodge in New Brunswick. (I told him it was probably Ted's idea.) And it was John-Henry who persisted in the burlesque of having Ted's body turned into a popsicle by a cryonics lab in Arizona. An object, it would seem, for further exploitation.

Certainly it was obvious to anyone who got close enough that John-Henry did those things for gain. (He drove Porsches, not Fords.) And when he died of leukemia less than two years after Ted's passing, I received more than a few calls suggesting it was "good riddance."

But I see it a little differently than that. Because from Ted's perspective, even if it was a mixed blessing, his son's return to his life was still, well, a blessing. Even in his diminished state, Williams was aware. He knew the young man was doing things, or at least had an inkling. "A pain in the ass," he said. "A pain-in-the-ass! But he's here for me. And I love him. And I think he loves me. I *know* he loves me." One of these days, he said, "I hope he marries that little girlfriend he's got now and they'll have a family, too. I hope to God he does."

But it should be remembered that this was right at the end, when Williams had made peace all around and was being unanimously hailed (and welcomed, *especially* in Boston) as nothing less than the iconic man. When we had first come together for the *SI* series years before, he was still struggling through the aftershocks of all that angst and bitterness. He said then that he realized he "should have had more fun in baseball than anyone who ever lived," but he hadn't, because he was "in a shell an awful lot, feeling sorry for myself, resenting things." He was a walking storehouse of resentments. And that had not ended with his escape from San Diego. Just the opposite.

Which brings us to Williams' tortured, career-long conflict with the Boston press, and the love-hate relationship with the Boston fans that sprang from it.

It was a wound of a subject Ted didn't have to be prodded to open in those first conversations in Ocala, and he freely admitted his own part in creating it. He said he arrived in the big leagues with a ton of baggage, and no doubt "things got started and grew worse because of my temperament, because of my emotional nature. I've never been a man with great patience." Consumed with making good at the one thing he felt he *could* make good at, he had no patience at all with himself. "I was impetuous, I was tempestuous. I blew up. I'd get so damned mad, throw bats, kick the columns in the dugout so that sparks flew, tear out the plumbing, knock out the lights, damn near kill myself. *Scream.* I'd scream out of my own frustration."

He told of a time in Minneapolis, the year before he went to the Red Sox, when he should have been finally at peace with the world, having found a seat on top of it. He was into a season ballplayers of any age dream of. "I led the American Association in everything—runs, average, RBIs, homers, everything. I had a wonderful manager, Donie Bush, who put up with me. The town was mine, and I loved it."

In the end, he at least came around to a better appreciation of the Boston fans, even to deciding, lo and behold, they were "the greatest in baseball."

He showed me the scars on his wrist from what happened. In a game against St. Paul, in the first inning, with the bases loaded, he got the pitch he wanted—a fastball, waist-high. "If I'd gotten that much more bat on the ball I'd have hit it 440 feet, but I popped it up. The St. Paul first baseman reached into the boxes and made a hell of a catch. Boy, I'm mad now. I go back to the bench, this little wooden bench, little crackerbox dugout in Minneapolis, and I'm so mad I don't know what to do. I sit down and here's this big water cooler right there next to me. About half full. And I just can't contain myself. *Whoomph.* I hit it with my fist. *Kerr-rash.* Sounded like a cannon had gone off in the dugout. It just exploded. Blood's flying, glass, everything.

"Well, I was lucky I didn't cut my hand off. There was one cut that went pretty deep"—he pointed to the scar—"and just missed a nerve. You don't have to cut very much there to do real damage. I could have ended my career before it started. As it was, the cut wasn't even bad enough to take me out of the game. But that shows you how intense I was."

So off to Boston the tempest flew, and for the first year reveled in more successes. He led the American League in RBIs with 145, and batted .327. "The fans in right field [at Fenway Park] were yelling for me all the time, and that year nobody tipped or waved his hat more than I did. I mean, right off my head, by the button. Nothing put on, nothing acted, just spontaneous. The next year things began to change, and I never did it again."

The change came with the souring of his relationship with the Boston press, and the animosities that spread from there into the stands. And I admit that when he first told me about it, I was skeptical. I had made only a cursory examination of the way he'd been treated in print and of the writers' "attitude" toward him, and thought his complaints overdrawn. Sports heroes, like rock stars, bellyache all the time about "coverage," especially if they are prone to controversial acts. Williams himself admitted that he had been "a fresh kid, doing a lot of yakking, partly to hide my inferiority complex. When somebody asked a question, I answered it. Never very coy, never very diplomatic. As a result I'd get myself in a wringer, and I'd say to myself, 'Damn, I wish I hadn't said that,' or said it that way, and sure as hell when I picked up the paper it was even worse than I meant."

So I thought for sure that when I took a closer look it would be his thin skin that would show through instead of a concerted bias. He had said, after all, that "in a crowd of cheers, I could always pick out the solitary boo."

But I was wrong. He had a few friends in the media even then that he could trust (more or less), but the more "influential" Boston columnists regularly trashed him. You read their comments now, against the historical evidence of his contributions to the game, and you have to call it nothing less than character assassination.

When he talked about it, Williams said he *still* remembered the things they wrote, "and they still make me mad: how I was always trying to get somebody's job, the manager's, the general manager's, the guy's in the radio booth—and I never coveted another man's job in my life. Or how I didn't hit in the clutch, and yet I drove in almost as many runs per time at bat as Babe Ruth, and my on-base percentage was better than anybody's, including Babe Ruth's. I was a 'draft dodger' [he served with distinction as a Marine pilot in two wars]. I wasn't a 'team' man. I was 'jealous.' I 'alienated the players from the press.' I 'didn't hit to left field.' I 'took too many bases on balls.' I did this, I did that. And so on, and so unfair."

He was savvy enough even then to see the dynamics of what was happening, though it didn't make him feel any better. Boston was overrun with newspapers ("more per capita than any place in the world," Williams said), their writers "all trying to outdo each other, all trying to get a headline, all digging into places where they had no business being. One of them sent a private detective to San Diego in 1942 to find out if I really did support my mother. [He received a one-year deferment before entering WWII.] They went into the street to take a 'public opinion' poll on my parental qualifications in 1948 when I happened to be away fishing when my daughter Bobby-Jo was born—prematurely. That type of thing."

His legion of detractors included the lead Boston columnists, Harold Kaese, Bill Cunningham, Huck Finnegan, and, worst of all in terms of being the most acerbic, Dave Egan of the *Boston Record*, known as "the Colonel," who seemed to have made castigating Ted Williams his life's work. Egan said Babe Ruth "could spit farther than Ted Williams could hit a baseball." He said Williams was "the most overrated buffoon in the history" of the game. He never let up.

> *He got away with bad behavior because he was allowed to get away with it, over and over, and eventually it became a lifestyle.*

And the Boston management? Williams was right about that, too. Privately and personally, they were warmly supportive (manager Cronin, owner Yawkey); publicly, they took a pass. Through his turmoil, they were quiet as mice. Let the prodigal sweat. Let him twist in the wind. It's news. It's *bringing people to the park*, if in some cases only to boo him. It was forever so, even when the detractors began to die off and Ted was into the twilight of his career. In 1957, when as "an old man who'd turned 39 in August" he hit .388 (the highest average in the major leagues since his supernal .406 in 1941), he "spent the season being mad at the world for one reason or another. I don't think I said two words to the Boston writers all year."

In the end, he at least came around to a better appreciation of the Boston fans, even to deciding, lo and behold, they were "the greatest in baseball." And he saw the irony in that, too (how could he not?). "Yeah, old Teddy Ballgame loved those fans all right. He spat at them and made terrible gestures at them and threw a bat that conked a nice old lady on the head one day, and he never tipped his hat to their cheers. And if you said that you'd be right." But he said there came a time "when I realized they were for me, when I knew, I *knew* they were for me, and how much it meant to me."

But he never apologized for his feelings about the Boston press. Those feelings hadn't changed. When feted in ceremonies before his very last game in 1960, he made a point when he got his turn at the microphone to reference "the terrible things" that had been written about him "by the Knights of the Keyboard." He lifted his gaze and gave the press box one final glare.

But how did all this factor into Ted Williams the man? He had endured most of his life's defining moments in combat zones—in San Diego, in Boston, in World War II, in Korea— and wound up being . . . what? Depictions then and since would have you believe he went out thumbing his nose at everything in sight: his critics, to be sure, but to every other order in his life as well. Having become too quickly a star apart, he seemed to have decided he wouldn't concern himself with societal restrictions, dress, or decorum; that he would do as he pleased, not only to take advantage of his celebrity status, but to live down to his notoriety. If he had been painted as a slob, living outside the lines, then that's damn well where he'd live and what he'd be.

I saw it manifest in many ways. Once, at the Ocean Reef Club where he almost bought a house but backed out when he realized there were rules to cope with, I took him to lunch in the crowded club dining room (not your average hole-in-the-wall). He paid no heed to the glances as we came in and while we ordered and were served. And with the practiced indifference of an upper-cruster, he casually stuffed his cloth napkin in the V-neck of his Ban-Lon shirt, cowboy-at-the-campfire fashion, and when he was near the bottom of his bowl of clam chowder, put aside his spoon and drank from the bowl. He got glances for that, too. He ignored them.

But what had convinced me almost from the start that he was unwilling to conform was his language. His flagrant, scathing use of invective, epithet, profanity, and blasphemy. In those many hours of conversation, I decided, upon returning to the scorched tapes for reference, that his abuses of Mother English were inveterate. I wasn't concerned about it originally; I didn't really mind. I've spent more than my share of time in barracks and locker rooms, and nothing really shocks me any more (not even at the movie theater). But whenever he got on to something that *really* irritated him, no matter where we were or who we were with, he took it to the extreme. I got a call from the secretary I hired to transcribe the tapes the day after I gave them to her. She said, in a halting voice, "I'm not sure I can do this. His cursing is . . . well, it really goes over the line."

It was true, of course. Williams was a world-class swearer. And a brilliant, almost poetic one at that, with verbal artistic renderings that might include five or six profanities in a row to cover all parts of speech (noun, adjective, verb, adverb, etc.) and complete a perfectly cogent sentence without a single polite word.

Moreover, he could be funny with it, even as he shocked you. One night when he came up from the Keys to dinner I also invited a tennis buddy of mine, Felix Baker, who later joined us on the courts a couple times. We had gathered at the bar, and Ted gave Baker a quizzical look and asked, "What did you say your name was?"

"Felix."

"Geezuz," Ted said, grimacing. "That's a shitty name."

Felix didn't recoil or act offended. He laughed. So did Ted. Somehow it hadn't come across as insulting at all. Jeannie Baker, then Felix' wife, was there. She was also the realtor who brought Ted and me several good real estate deals. She said after Ted died that she didn't recall his cursing at all, only that "he talked so loud the pictures on the wall shook."

The batter's box was his holy of holies. There you did not challenge the higher authority; you bowed to it.

I asked Williams once, when we were waiting on something to pass our way in a duck blind, why he felt the need to use such language, his being so articulate otherwise, with a perfectly serviceable vocabulary. He said that when he got mad and couldn't stand it, "when I get pissed and have to speak out," he couldn't help himself, and "I have absolutely no repentance. . . . I wake up some nights and I'm mad about something and I let off . . . steam, and at that point I don't care if I go to hell or burn. I know I've tried to do things basically right, even though I've done a lot of things I'm terribly ashamed of, too, but I feel in my heart if you laid it all out, I've been on the right side [most of the time]. . . . But sometimes I have to say, 'Fuck it.' And I feel better when I do."

So I had to conclude that the condition was chronic. Then something happened that changed my mind about that, too. I had seen him move easily in the company of owners and politicians and various "big shots" (his words) without sounding all that offensive, and when the book on his life (*My Turn at Bat*, following the series in *SI*) made the bestseller lists, we were invited by Hedley Donovan to the Time-Life Building for a commemorative luncheon. I said yes to their request to have us speak to the group, though I admit to having second thoughts when Ted got up. I stood at the back of the room, my palms moist, and watched him captivate a roomful of magazine editors with a 10-minute, off-the-cuff speech that included nary a "hell" or a "damn." I thought, "How about that."

The hard truth, of course, is that the antiestablishmentarianism and childish acts he carried into adulthood were not as complicated as his apologists (or his critics) made it seem. Underlying influences aside, he got away with bad behavior because he was *allowed* to get away with it, over and over, and eventually it became a lifestyle. Ironically, the sainted Yawkey, from the old school of ownership that didn't regard players as "labor" but as children, was exactly the kind of indulgent father Ted never had, and didn't need. From those first years, Yawkey spoiled Williams rotten. For his tantrums, the Kid was not rebuked, he was rewarded. He was never made to suffer for his transgressions. It wasn't complicated at all.

So *could* Williams have been disciplined? Of course. The proof can be found not in his inconsistencies, but in his consistencies: in those vital segments of his life where he demonstrated the utmost control—and where he rigidly disciplined himself. Consider, first, his hitting. The lifeblood of his expression. Nothing in sport, he believed, required more skill, more scientific application and control, and if he didn't make it as "the greatest hitter who ever lived," his dream from childhood, the case could be made that he was certainly the most disciplined. Those who were dumbfounded when he so passively deferred to the authority of umpires, never arguing called strikes or making a scene, should not have been. The batter's box was his holy of holies. There you did not challenge the higher authority; you bowed to it.

When I asked him about the "umpires thing"—as it had been routinely referred to, derisively, by the media—Ted said he knew the public didn't get his "unnatural serenity" around umpires. The writers he blew up at and the fans he hollered at never seemed to understand it. Baseball's traditional bullseyes Ted Williams never rebuked, never complained about. He said it was simple: "I never doubted their sincerity, I never doubted their integrity. Some were better than others, some controlled the game better, but all of them were a dedicated bunch of guys, gung-ho, a special breed that made umpiring a life's calling. The mistakes they made were *always* honest mistakes as far as I'm concerned—heat of the battle, spur of the moment things. The things I reacted to were opinionated, thought-out, written-out lies."

But the last thing that convinced me—and would have already convinced anyone who knew him or read about him had they stopped to think about—was something I didn't really put in focus until our last time together. The fact that he had been, by all the evidence, an exemplary Marine officer. A first-rate jet pilot. A war hero in Korea. If he resented being there, as he said he did when sent because he was practically into middle-age and felt

He said when people asked to know "a little bit about me," in the way of summarizing, "I say, 'I was a Marine.'"

he was being "used by the politicians," he went uncomplaining, smart enough to know that in that environment, a lack of discipline would never be tolerated, and might even get him killed. He thrived on it.

The equivalent of five baseball seasons were taken out of his career by Ted Williams' service as a Marine. No other player in the history of the game made so calculable a sacrifice. On that last visit to Hernando, when he was noticeably enfeebled by the strokes and probably should have been resting, Ted insisted that we stay longer than we should have, and it seemed by his actions that it was mainly so that he could regale Josh with stories about his experiences in "the Corps."

He moved us into a huge den, with full-size portraits and trophies and memorabilia all around, and while Caroline captured the moment with a video camera, Ted showed Josh pictures of his Marine exploits, and told him about being shot down in Korea. He gave him the full load: the mission, the attack, the ordnance involved, his eventual crash landing. He said his favorite song, right behind "God Bless America," was "The Marine Hymn." He said when people asked to know "a little bit about me," in the way of summarizing, "I say, 'I was a Marine.'"

And as he talked, I glanced down and realized that I was standing on a plush, cream-colored rug that had as its embroidered centerpiece a giant, multicolored replica of the Marine insignia.

And I realized the something that should have been impressed on me a long time ago if I'd been more aware. That you can't be indifferent about your conduct and be a Marine, or be cavalier about your dress or your language. That you can't be a slob and be a Marine.

Said Ted Williams: "It was the best team I ever played for."

CHAPTER 4

A Vindication, of Sorts

THE PULSE OF THE RIVER CAME to the tent at night on muffled, even steps, like an army tiptoeing. Ordinarily, I would have been asleep in minutes. Whenever in the wild and at the mercy of its discord, I think of water moving audibly nearby as a surefire sleep inducer, even in Africa where the ambiance might include the *whoop-whoop* of a passing hyena or the ominous cough of a lion. Except now, by the Kafue River in Zambia, on safari, languishing on cots long past Ted Williams' bedtime, I had the prattle of Williams himself to keep me awake. The happiest Ted Williams I have ever known.

It began months before and an ocean removed when, under false pretenses, he had taken the job of managing the moribund Washington Senators (eventually the Texas Rangers). For public consumption, he said on the day he committed that the only thing that could possibly have gotten him off his big fat tackle box and back into baseball where he belonged was "money . . . m-o-n-e-y.

I haven't got it made yet. It may look like I have, I'm close, but I'm not fixed financially. This might be the way." And as if to further embrace the credo of modern American sport: "Let's face it, there's a price for everything."

But that night when he sliced into the thick sirloin steak he had brought to my house for the occasion (and broiled on the grill himself, without asking to be asked) and examined his feelings further, he put them into a quite different perspective. The one I knew better, including the obvious: that he didn't need more money to do the things he loved to do. He said he had fished and hunted uninhibited for almost nine years, since retiring as a player after the 1960 season. As much as he appreciated such an idyllic life, he said, it amounted to an awful lot of time spent on his rear end.

He said that baseball, after all, remained his first love, and he had all those convictions lying around collecting dust. He had been only on its fringes for eight seasons—as a batting coach for young Red Sox players in the spring, a job he had found increasingly unrewarding. He thought it was time he quit wasting his opinions on the walls. And, of course, as the first and best reason to give it a whirl, he said it would allow him to provide the Senators access to his storehouse of knowledge on "the single most difficult thing to do in sport," hitting a baseball. We had, in fact, just finished his book on the subject.

I asked him, finally, about "that other thing," the lingering hurt, long obscured from the public eye, of having never been asked to manage the Red Sox. He reminded me that he *had* been asked, actually, when he was near the end of his playing career "and the team was lousy and going nowhere." But he told owner Tom Yawkey then that he still had some hitting to do and declined. After that, he said he felt "there was a faction [within the Boston organization] that undercut me a little, that didn't want me around, maybe out of jealousy. I never felt I was really wanted, so I said the hell with it." He admitted, however, that he really hadn't been all that approachable on the subject, that toward the end, whenever Yawkey asked him what he wanted to do

> *He said on the day he committed that the only thing that could possibly have gotten him off his big fat tackle box and back into baseball where he belonged was "money . . . m-o-n-e-y."*

when he quit playing, "I'd always tell him I'd like to do *something*, but I sure as hell didn't want to manage."

Ironically, when the Washington Senators' one-man campaign to get him was proceeding apace (the man being the team owner, Bob Short), and Williams was insisting over and over that he knew nothing about managing—that, while he appreciated the offer, Short should get someone else—Ted got a call from Joe Cronin, his first manager in Boston. Cronin was then the president of the American League. He pleaded with Ted to take the job. He said the league needed him. *Baseball* needed him.

The second irony was in the personage of Bob Short himself. Or, more accurately, Short's willingness, as a tactic, to persist in the face of Williams' fortress-like reluctance. Tom Yawkey, gentleman owner that he was, didn't have it in him to plow through all that rejection. Short ignored it. The millionaire businessman out of Minneapolis and former chairman of the Democratic Party had gotten Ted's phone number from a mutual friend and engaged him in a series of long distance calls, making his case.

> *Whenever Yawkey asked him what he wanted to do when he quit playing, "I'd always tell him I'd like to do something, but I sure as hell didn't want to manage."*

Williams returned a couple of them from my den in Miami. He said, "I keep saying 'no' until I hear myself saying 'yes.'" Bob Short, he said, "is the smartest man I ever met." At the art of sizing people up, Williams was a first-impressionist.

At that point he conceded that if baseball needed him, he very well might still need it. He said, "This may be my last real chance to get back into the game on my own terms." Bob Short, for sure, had reached his wavelength, partly by charming him to death. (He told Ted how, as a teenager in Minneapolis when the teenaged Ted played there in 1938, he "wore holes in my pants sitting on the bleachers watching you hit.") He thus was able to talk Ted into doing something no one else had been able to, and to manage the adynamic Senators, which no one would *want* to do without the kind of contract baseball managers didn't get at the time. Which is what Ted got.

The next day he flew up to meet with Short and sign on. The total package was for more than $1.25 million, huge money then (Williams was hailed as baseball's "first million-dollar manager"). It called for him to manage five years. Stock would be put aside so that over a 10-year period he could wind up with 10 percent of the club. And he had an out. If after the first year he decided he was right all along—that managing a baseball team was an aggravation beyond his endurance—then he could kick himself upstairs, to be general manager or whatever he thought would serve the club best. And if he wanted to quit after that and go back to the Keys, to Dolores and John-Henry and his fishing boat, he could do that, too.

All those things so that Short could provide on a platter the biggest name imaginable for the Washington fans to feed on. Except that it was a movable feast, and all of baseball partook. I went to Pompano, Florida, the first week he was there for spring training, and I never saw so many smiles. Ted was having a ball, abject misgivings notwithstanding. When we were alone in his cubbyhole of an office at the little park, he rummaged through a stack of letters and produced one he said had arrived just that morning. He said it provided a full analysis, from a "trusted old baseball friend," typewritten front and back on a single sheet of yellow copy paper. It alerted Ted to the "terrible mistake" he was making. "I was wondering if I was making a mistake," he laughed.

He read the letter aloud. It said that the Washington team was the worst in the majors, with the worst organization, the worst scouting system, the worst minor league talent. The Senators didn't draw; their stadium was in a riot area. Managing them would put him in contact with sportswriters. Sportswriters would bring up "that old bull they always bring up." He would have to do public relations. He would be asked a million stupid questions, and would develop an ulcer. He would have a strict schedule. No time off. No way to run away and hide. He would have to wet-nurse 25 ballplayers, not all adults. Losses would be on *his* record; on *his* reputation. He would go into Boston as an enemy, against his old benefactor, Tom Yawkey. He would discover—at age 50—that he could still hit better than any player on his team, and would be sorely tempted to pinch-hit.

"'The Washington players need years of coaching, not days,'" Williams read, and laughed again. "'Frank Howard will kill your sensibilities as a batter. His strikeouts on bad pitches will have you talking to yourself all night.'" He hurried to the end and smiled when he read: "'The Washington boys need to be reborn, not remade.'" The friend's conclusion was that he had "never known a happy manager." He advised Ted to reconsider.

Ted did not reconsider, of course. And it was wrong to have assumed (as some suggested) that he came back just for the applause, and maybe some of the beatification he'd had to do without in Boston. The intensities that made him a great hitter and allowed him to examine himself with such ruthless candor were still there, and refreshingly so. The new, agreeable Ted was still Ted Williams, just nine years older, wiser, a bit more refined and—for this new chapter in his life—infinitely more aware of the responsibilities of his position than when he last made black headlines in Boston.

The voyage of rediscovery began with a car ride up from the Keys to Pompano that I shared with him. He said he'd made up his mind to be dead serious about "this business of managing," a business he had more or less belittled for years. He did not pack a fishing rod; he did not carry a golf club or tennis racquet.

"I'm going to try," he said in the car. "I may turn out to be a horseshit manager, but I'm going to *try*. I'm going to be the last man out on that field every day if that will help. I'm going to do whatever it takes for this guy [Short].

He read the letter aloud. It said that the Washington team was the worst in the majors, with the worst organization, the worst scouting system, the worst minor league talent.

"I know my weaknesses. I don't know infield play, that's my special little bugaboo. I don't know how to run a game, at least I don't feel I do. I never even made a lineup card. It's something I don't know about—when to do certain things, when to make changes. Get too interested watching a pitcher or a batter and you're two moves behind before you know it. But I'll have somebody right beside me helping me with that part of the act. The thing I know about, the most important part of baseball, is that game between the batter and the pitcher. Nobody knows that better than me. I *know* I'm going to be able to help those hitters. And the pitchers, too. I'm sure of it."

Through the spring, he made no attempt to hide the doubts that surfaced. "You know what can scare you?" he said one night at the home he rented in Fort Lauderdale so that Dolores and the infant John-Henry could join him at camp. "The rules. I've been reading this book about problems that have come up over rules. So you think you know baseball? Boy. You wouldn't believe the things you find in here. It can scare you." What gratified him, he said, was that "the kids are trying. They're really working hard." He said he ordered a midnight curfew, no serious card playing, no players in the hotel bar. Get drunk, get fined. Nobody complained. He had Joe McCarthy's "10 Commandments of Baseball" posted for reference, pushing such encouragements as: "Nobody ever became a ballplayer by walking after a ball," and, "Do not alibi on bad hops, anybody can field the good ones."

By the end of spring training, the makeover was in place. And the Washington team not only responded, it was . . . well, yes, reborn. It produced the franchise's first winning season in 24 years, going well over .500 at 86–76, a 21-game improvement over the previous season. Ted's theories on hitting, and the practical application thereof, proved eminently transmittable. The Senators went from an abysmal .224 team batting average in 1968 to .251 in 1969, and its lineup of strugglers morphed into varying forms of respectability.

Eddie Brinkman, the good-field/no-hit shortstop who choked up so far on the bat that Williams said he wasn't sure which end he was trying to hit with, raised his average almost a hundred points, from .187 to .267. ("I knew he was a better hitter than his record indicated from the moment I saw him," Ted said.) Hank Allen went from .219 to .267; Del Unser from .230 to .286; Ken McMullen from .248 to .272; Frank Howard hit .296 with 48 home runs; and Mike Epstein (from seasons of

.226 and .234) hit .278—the best years they ever had in the big leagues. Ted's pitchers profited from his teaching, too; they discovered they could throw strikes. Dick Bosman had the lowest earned-run average in the league.

Baseball fans embraced him in D.C. and everywhere he went that year, including Boston. The Senators' home attendance almost doubled, revenues almost tripled. He was the eye of an unrelenting hurricane of attention, almost always the most applauded, sometimes the *only* applauded. From the edges of the field and off it, he enjoyed the benediction of a doting, if not downright compliant, media. In their presence he managed to keep being the Unterrible Teddy everybody had come to adore in Pompano. The aces of American sports journalism, honored men like Shirley Povich of the *Washington Post* and Arthur Daley of the *New York Times*, sang his praises in bravura. Ralph Houk of the Yankees said that one Yankees official had complained in the spring that Ted had taken all the writers and photographers away from the other camps. "Listen," Ted chirped when he heard it, "you can have them all back."

Moreover, he had done it not with mirrors but with hard work and an intellectual application that many doubted he was capable of. And he did it without diatribe or controversy. He broke no bats (well, a couple), popped no vocal chords yelling at fans, intimidated no journalists with his acid tongue. He suffered their scrutiny as well as any diplomat—if you overlook the times he corrected dumb questions with, as he put it, "polite instruction." When questions lagged at postgame press conferences, he asked a few himself. He was, in every way imaginable, a model citizen, and a contented man.

When the season was over, Bud Morgan of ABC invited him to go to Africa—to Zambia—to hunt sable antelope for an *American Sportsman* television special. Ted called and invited me along. Actually, he insisted. He said he was tired of hearing stories about my adventures in Africa (he'd never been) and wanted to see if I could hit the broad side of an elephant, or preferably something smaller. I told him I was hoping he'd ask, and packed my bags.

On the way over, it was more of the same. Our first stop was in London, and when I took him to the Tower of London (he hadn't been there, either), an American boy, holding a camera with both hands, shadowed him through the tour and then waited 40 minutes outside Coldharbour Gate as Williams inspected 17th-century glaives and wheel-lock pistols and browsed through the tilt armor. "Now, Mr. Williams?" the boy said when Ted emerged, and was granted a friendly pose. In Nairobi, an old man in canvas shoes and a soiled shamba hat stepped in front of him and said, "Hey, you're Ted Williams!"

"A lot of people make that mistake," Ted said, a response he used often to deflect attention. "I think Williams is actually an older man."

"Aw, c'mon, I saw you *play*, Ted. You know. In Boston. In *Boston*. Oh, how I'd love to be in Boston."

"People I know want to come here."

"Ted, you gotta tell me," said the man in the shamba. "Did the Mets really win the Series? You know"—he looked around conspiratorially—"you can't believe everything you read out here."

"Yeah, the Mets won, all right. Four games to one [over the Orioles]."

"Mmmm. Please. Tell me about it." The man was starved for information, and Williams obliged him with a five-minute report.

At a five and dime, the discovery was made by an Episcopal missionary in from Tanzania. The missionary introduced his son, whom he quickly acquainted with Williams' accomplishments. The man and the boy seemed

He broke no bats (well, a couple), popped no vocal chords yelling at fans, intimidated no journalists with his acid tongue. He suffered their scrutiny as well as any diplomat.

immensely pleased to have him drop in on their continent.

"How did Frank Howard do this year?" the missionary wanted to know. "Is he still swinging at bad pitches? I saw him when I was home on leave a few years ago. Swung from his heels at everything."

"No," Ted assured him. "Howard doesn't do that as much anymore."

Between soup and salad that night at the New Stanley Hotel, Williams elaborated on the corrections he'd made in Howard's hitting habits. He said they were not exactly secrets if "Episcopalians in Africa were spreading the word. That oughta tell you how obvious it was. It was obvious the first time I saw him play years ago with the Dodgers in a World Series. I knew when I took this job exactly what I was gong to say to him. The value of knowing the strike zone. The value of proper thinking at the plate. The importance of getting a good ball to hit. Of knowing when not to be too big with his swing.

It is around the campfires in Africa the best stories are told, sometimes augmented by the liquid mixes brought to the circle by camp attendants before the evening meal, and most of the talk there was about the hunting itself.

"We talked whenever we had a chance, and I want to tell you, Frank Howard is a wonderful guy. A *great* guy. We analyzed his bases on balls—only 54 last year, and 12 of those were intentional. Well, for crying out loud, the *leadoff* man should get 35 walks. Howard didn't know the strike zone. It was as simple as that."

"So how many times did he walk this year?" I asked.

"One hundred and two. And he cut his strikeouts by one-third, and his average was higher than ever, and he *still* hit more home runs, some of them out of sight. I mean he *crushed* the ball. I think without question he's the biggest, strongest guy who ever played this game."

His voice had risen, and the people at the next table, who had been folded over their meals, were now listening in and whispering behind their hands. One of them finally leaned in and offered Williams a menu.

"Would you sign this, Mr. Williams?" he said. "Never thought I'd run into you way out here. Uh, just make it out to, uh, 'Theodore Samuel.'"

"Great name," said Williams, taking the menu.

The man laughed self-consciously. "Yes, it's for my nephew. My brother named him after you. My brother is a real nut."

"Gee, thanks a lot," said Williams, feigning hurt. "Thanks a lot."

(For the record, the "Samuel" in Williams' full name was never on his birth certificate. His parents didn't give him a middle name. He added it himself later, by choice, "because I thought it sounded good.")

On the flight out of Nairobi, the discovery was made by the man in the seat ahead of us. He got up on his knees and turned around to offer himself for conversation. Eventually he asked Williams what made a good manager.

"To have enthusiasm," Ted said. "To *show* enthusiasm, not just in a game but from spring training on. To be on top of it every minute. Then, *then*, to know enough to have guys around you who can help a guy—who can teach a guy. That's a key. There's very little really good teaching done in baseball today. I'm convinced of that.

"So, if you have that, and if you have that little extra that Casey Stengel could get out of a team, and you've got good pitching—well, that's where it pays off. You talk about the great teams and they *always* had good pitching. The Yankees.

Cleveland. The pitching kept them in the close games. Then, in the late innings, boom, something happened, and they won."

"And a manager makes this happen?"

"He can. He can. But in a variety of ways. I'm keyed up all the time, trying to keep guys alert, asking questions, trying to get them to think. It's my nature. But I watched Gil Hodges [the Mets manager] in the Series, sitting in the dugout, arms crossed. Never changed position. But he had enthusiastic coaches and a young club full of life, and—*and*—he had a businesslike attitude, and a team has to have that, too. The kind of attitude Joe McCarthy always instilled in a team. McCarthy never made a big scene.

"The Mets had another thing important to an organization. They had people who were willing to spend money. (They) went out and bought what was necessary, and guys were getting paid and that makes for a good atmosphere. And I'll tell you something else. I wouldn't be surprised if the Mets kept winning for a long time."

We were in Lusaka, at midnight. We had just checked into our hotel as the final stop before heading out the next morning for the bush, when Ted got a call in our room. Bob Addie of the *Washington Post*, persevering through the labyrinth of overseas traffic, had big news: Williams had been named Manager of the Year in the American League.

"Boy, just like the Russian secret police," Williams shouted, teasing Addie for tracking him down. "Are you sure? . . . Unh-hnh. . . . Well, yes, I'm flabbergasted, Bob. But I'll tell you something. It was just another example of the writers being wrong again. [Earl] Weaver and [Billy] Martin deserved it more. I'm happy for myself, but I feel bad for them."

"I honestly feel that way," he said when he hung up, and there with him, I had no doubt he meant it. "I'm a Johnny-Come-Lately in this business, and those guys won their divisions, and Weaver won the pennant in a breeze. I voted for Weaver. If you win like he did and don't get it, well . . . "

It was cool and overcast at the main campsite on the Kafue River when we joined the other ABC conscripts for the sports-man show. Each was there to film a segment on hunting a specific animal. It was a congenial grouping we both immedi-ately liked and came to enjoy, although neither of the other two principals, Cliff Robertson, the actor who had starred as John F. Kennedy in *PT-109*, and Don Meredith, the quarterback who had starred for the Dallas Cowboys before repairing to the tele-vision booth as a color man for *Monday Night Football*, had the hunting expertise of Ted Williams. Meredith, in fact, had brought his pretty wife along and suggested she was the one with the itchy trigger-finger and should be doing the segment. Ms. Meredith obviously loved the outdoors; Meredith seemed more to tolerate it. He kidded that he'd just as soon have stayed in Lusaka for the "nightlife."

The October rainy season was bearing down on the Zambian veldt when we went out the next day. We hunted in separate directions, with different guides, and then converged at night by the campfire to share what we'd experienced. It is around the campfires in Africa the best stories are told, sometimes augmented by the liquid mixes brought to the circle by camp attendants before the evening meal, and most of the talk there was about the hunting itself.

> *His first shot slammed into the shoulder of the buffalo, which hunched up and spun groggily in a tight arc, seeking the source of its torment. Williams then put a second bullet through its septum.*

Williams brought down his designated prey, the sable antelope, almost as soon as we arrived (I didn't get close enough to one to consider it until the very last day, and shot it, somewhat reluctantly, in the rain). When the pressure of performing that task on-camera was off, Ted went out for others, and shot well—reedbuck, warthog, impala for camp meat, et al. But what he wanted most to hunt was Cape buffalo, one of Africa's "big five" that he'd heard me talk about often, usually in the form of unabashed boasting. I had gotten one in Botswana, hunting on the edge of the Kalahari Desert and Okavanga Swamp with Harry Selby, the storied Mau-Mau fighter from Kenya whom Robert Ruarke had written about in *Something of Value* years before. When Ted got a chance after the sable antelope shoot, he took it. I wasn't with him, but he gladly filled us in around the campfire.

He had brought it down while the sun was high, in a place virtually free of cover except for isolated thorn bushes and a few clumps of mapone scrub. To get close enough, he'd had to crawl on his belly through the rutted spoor of elephants that had passed over the veldt during the last rainy season and left ruptured earth to harden into craters under the sun. "Geezus, I musta dragged that .458 a hundred-fifty yards," he said. "My elbows and knees were grinding into the elephant tracks. I was thinking maybe we'd made a bad decision."

He said when he got into a sitting position with the .458, pressing his elbows inside his knees for stability, he wasn't sure he could control his breathing enough to stay on target. But his first shot slammed into the shoulder of the buffalo, which hunched up and spun groggily in a tight arc, seeking the source of its torment. Williams then put a second bullet through its septum. The third shot was as redundant as the second.

He was tired and relieved when he returned to camp with Rolf Rohwer, an American on the professional staff of Zambia Safaris Inc., and the mood of urgency had left him. His clothes were dirt-crusted and his beard was patchy with dust, and he was an altogether contented man. He made a show of moaning over the aches he had accumulated crawling through the ruts. He massaged his left shoulder and complained that Rohwer, whom he called "Ralph" (Williams was shameless for putting his own spin on proper names), did not suffer equally. "Damnit, Ralph," he said, "you got to hurt somewhere." And then he smiled. "Boy, I wanta tell you. That buffalo hunting is the fun."

And with that he retired to the tent for the rest of the afternoon, suggesting over his shoulder that he'd like to try for a "bigger horn" tomorrow.

Mike Cameron, another of the professional hunters Zambia Safaris had brought in for the group, watched him go from where we were sitting over a late lunch. Cameron had been with him, too, along with an old lion hunter named Johnny Uys who had actually been the one to put Williams in position near the buffalo herd. "He's pleased, your Mr. Williams is," Cameron said. "But he will not dream of the buffalo. He will dream of adding 50 percentage points to Mr. Casanova's batting figure— is that right, 'Casanova?' "

"Yes. Paul Casanova. A catcher," I said.

"Or how to make Mr. Coleman a better pitcher."

"How do you know all that?" I asked. (Only a few days before Ted had said: "I close my eyes and lie there thinking, 'How am I going to get to [Joe] Coleman? How am I going to get to this guy? What can I say without discouraging him?' He could be so much better. It's going to be my number one project next spring.")

"Because," said Cameron, "he is a magnificent fraud, your Ted. He is genuinely enthusiastic about everything. He argues about the strength of fishing line [we had talked about going for tiger fish in the Zambezi] and about ballistics, and he is very positive with his arguments, but I suspect he has only one true love, and he pretends to deny her.

"I asked him about managing," Cameron went on, "about getting back into baseball after all these years—we have baseball in Rhodesia [Zimbabwe], you know, so I know a little about it—and he said he would not be back at all if he had enough money and if he had a big boat like Zane Grey had and could sail the world. He could see himself saying, 'Boy, see you later.' I suspect that is a front."

When Ted emerged later it was for the interplay around the evening fire, where the pedigrees of the participants were so rich and varied that there was a constant flow of conversational show-stoppers. Nevertheless, Williams was mostly the center of it, and when Don Meredith asked him how he was able to effectively pick up in baseball where he left off after all those years, Ted said the truth was that things happened so fast he didn't realize how little prepared he really was.

He unloaded, and I resigned myself to it, since, in the bedlam hours that sometimes come before sleep in Africa, the toe frogs and night birds were into their usual hysterics.

"I'm signing, then I'm packing and going to camp, and I don't know who's on the team or anything. I remember talking to one of the Washington writers, trying to get some information, and he mentioned 'Hondo,' and I said, 'Gee, tell me about that Hondo. How good is he?' Well, Hondo is Frank Howard, but *I* didn't know that."

Cliff Robertson asked him if he'd enjoyed "coaching" the players, and Ted said he got a kick out of helping them improve, but that some of them "wouldn't listen, or were just too dumb to understand," and that tried his patience. They talked about patience for awhile, and Ted said he had "none" for anybody who wouldn't listen. He recalled how much patience he'd had with the young fighter pilots he helped train when he was preparing for combat in Korea; how he wouldn't give them "downs" for honest mistakes, "but how hard I was on guys coming back through as instructors who *thought* they were good and they weren't; who *thought* they knew what they were doing and didn't. I gave them downs. I expected more, and I didn't get it, and I gave 'em downs."

Meredith suggested that the Washington team's pitching evidently got better, but that it must not have been enough. "Everybody needs pitching," Ted said. "It's the oldest story in baseball. *Nobody* has enough."

We were interrupted at that point by an announcement from Johnny Uys that there were crocodiles nosing up to the edge of the river where camp attendants had put a heavy-duty screen fence in the water to form a make-do corral for swimming. Several of the film crew had jumped in and were splashing around. We went over to the river to look, and the crocodiles were there, all right, idling like submarines just below the surface and nudging the screen enclosure. Ted Williams grinned and said he really regretted leaving his swimming trunks at home.

Now, in the tent after hours, I was paying the price for not having joined him for an afternoon nap. Stretched out on his cot in a halo of light from a ridiculously full moon, he went on unprompted with his critique of the season he had promised would never happen. Except now he didn't bother to issue any of the polite disclaimers he felt necessary around the campfire. He unloaded, and I resigned myself to it, since, in the bedlam hours that sometimes come before sleep in Africa, the toe frogs and night birds were into their usual hysterics.

"Did you enjoy it? The season?" I asked, my eyes closed.

"I enjoyed being on the field," he said, and yawned such a loud, sustained yawn it seemed he, too, would not last the sentence through. "I enjoyed being with the players, helping them, working with them. You feel good when things are perking. There is no greater satisfaction I know of than when things are going well. When things aren't going well—"

He named a player who had not responded to stimuli, who had told Williams that all he really cared about was "lying on the beach in the sun somewhere." In Ted's mind's eye, he had to be seeing the young Ted Williams, practicing until the blisters bled. He said, "This guy just hasn't got it. He hasn't been out for extra hitting practice four times all year. That's what I mind. Well, he ain't going to be on our team, I don't believe, and still I don't know how we're going to get rid of him, we don't have anyone any better, and that's what bothers you on a club like this. Where do you go from here? It's going to be a struggle to improve."

There was a long pause, and I thought he was done, but he went on.

"This is the thing. If I was smart, if I was really smart, I'd say forget about it, see you later. I can see this is the kind of job you suffer with, you get a lousy ulcer, you get buried in it . . ."

The mood passed as quickly as it came. Williams was now tuned to the stimulus of laying his opinions out, and never mind conversation. He shifted on the cot ponderously, and then sat up. Not to look at me, but to better marshal his thoughts.

"The fun," he said, "was seeing them improve and realize they *could* win, and that's a satisfaction to me."

Yes, I said, but early on he was worried about having so much to learn. What about that?

"That's why I said Vince Lombardi [then coaching the Washington Redskins] showed me something. Here I'm starting out, not knowing what's going on, whether I can do it, who the coaches are, who the players are, what I'm getting into. And I look over there and I see where Lombardi has hired *head* coaches as his assistants, and, boy, that woke me up. The smartest coach in football has *head* coaches as his assistants. He *surrounds* himself with good guys. By the time spring training started, I'd made up my mind to do the same thing. I was going to get all the help I could get."

> *"A manager's got nine million lousy little things to do, things on his mind, people to see, lists to check, the press to fool with after the game, the press to fool with before the game, a million things"*

Again he shifted tacks.

"The big thing for me was the infield. It's probably true that a good infielder can help another infielder better than a batter can help another batter because there's certain set ways to do things in the infield, things I never knew because I'd never played infield. I was an outfielder."

"Like what?" I asked.

"Like bunting situations. For example, man on first, maybe hit-and-run or bunt coming. The guy at the plate turns to bunt and decides instead to hit away. Now,"—he was on the edge of the cot, framed by the moonlight against the mosquito-netting of the window—"say your head's home plate. I'm the second baseman. There's first. On a bunt, I'm supposed to break to first, to cover there. Fast. Break to first on the bunt. Well, the correct way to do it—and I never knew this—is for me, the second baseman, to take a step *in* toward you so that if the batter straightens up and tries to ram it through I'm still in position to make the play. *Then* if the guy bunts, I'm already moving and can turn toward first. Start *in*, then go to first. I didn't know that."

"So that's why you tried to hire Johnny Pesky?" I asked. Pesky, the former All-Star infielder, had been a teammate of Ted's with the Red Sox and was a close friend.

"Well, I had Foxie [Nellie Fox] all set as one of my coaches, but he couldn't do it all. I asked Pesky if he wanted to come, but he was tied up with television in Boston. I had Pat Mullin, but he was an outfielder. And I had Trahilliger."

"Terwilliger," I corrected.

"What?"

"Wayne Terwilliger. You pronounced it wrong in the spring, and you're still pronouncing it wrong. It's a wonder he stuck with you."

"Ter-will-i-ger." He sounded it out. "You're a wise guy, you know that? All right, just keep quiet and listen and maybe you'll learn something.

"Ter-will-i-ger was supposed to be the Buffalo manager. But when I got to know him at Pompano—a real pepper pot, always on top of things, always watching the guys—I said to myself, 'Boy, I want this guy.'

"Trahilliger had managed. And as we went along I said, 'Twig, you just run the game from third base, and if there's anything you want from the bench we'll let you know.' These things can work out when you've got a guy who can do the job, whether he's coaching first or third or in the bullpen. When he can do it, boom, let him do it. From a manager's viewpoint, it's the only smart way. A manager's got nine million lousy little things to do, things on his mind, people to see, lists to check, the press to fool with after the game, the press to fool with *before* the game, a million things."

"Were you worried about handling the press?"

"No, hell no. I couldn't have worried less. The only trouble I had was over the 15-minute rule: nobody allowed in the dressing room for 15 minutes after the game. I wanted to give the players a chance to be alone a little bit, and I got a few yowls over it. After about a month I got a little soft and said, well, I'll make it 10 minutes, trying to cooperate, and one of them kept bitching and bitching, so I said, 'It's going back to 15 minutes,' and the United States Congress ain't going to make me change.

"There are good guys in the Washington press, and we got along. I didn't get real chummy with any of them, but it's better not to get too close. They knew they could come to me and get some dope now and then, and when I thought they were off base, I told them so. The thing that bothered me a little was they were the last to believe in us. After a month and a half they were still writing, 'Gee, when are the Senators going to collapse?' So I had a little session with them one day, and I said,

'Look, everybody in this town thinks we're going to do it except you guys. You are the least impressed of anybody with this club. The least enthusiastic. For God's sake, wake up.' I'd give 'em the treatment whenever I could. Especially when I knew I was right."

He laughed and flopped back down on the cot. There was a long pause. I thought he might have drifted off, but then he was back from wherever he'd been.

But I think you could certainly argue the case that for that one season, from first pitch to last, he was the happiest he had ever been in baseball.

"The one big impression I got is that the game hasn't changed. It's the same as it was when I played. I see the same type pitchers, the same type hitters. I'm a little more convinced than ever that there aren't as many good hitters in the game, guys who can whack the ball around when it's over the plate, like an Aaron or a Clemente. There are plenty of guys with power, guys who hit the ball a long way, but I see so many who lack finesse, who should hit for average but don't."

He talked about players who had come to him for advice on hitting, even from opposing teams. When he played he had been the softest of touches for such entreaties. The Rocky Colavitos and the Al Kalines and the Moose Skowrons would come around, and he'd always oblige. This time, most notably, it was Ken Harrelson of the Indians, who Ted said was "cocking his hips prematurely, restricting the pendulum action of his swing." He made a grunting noise, causing me to open my eyes once more to find him up again, demonstrating Harrelson's mistakes. He flopped back down. The tricky part about helping in that case, he said, was that after taking his advice, Harrelson beat the Senators with a home run. He said he'd have to be more selective with his prescriptions.

"Listen," he said, calling it a night at last. "Did you zip up your side of the tent? I don't want any snakes in here. When it comes to snakes, I'm no hero." The night before it had been the bugs that bothered him. He put up such a fog of bug spray that it settled wet on our foreheads. Sometimes now when I'm having trouble sleeping I blame it on the residue from all that spray.

The hunting dried up after the buffalo shoot. Williams scoured the hills away from the river with young Rolf Rohwer. He especially liked Rohwer, a tireless, meticulous professional, and thought nothing of engaging him in the merciless kidding that he conferred on his friends.

One afternoon I told him, in Rolf's presence, "Listen, you've got to start calling people by their right names. Like calling Terwilliger 'Trahilliger' all season."

"No, I didn't," Ted replied. "I called him 'Twig' most of the time."

"And it's not 'Ralph,' it's 'Rolf.'"

"What? Well, you can say it the way you want. I believe in pronouncing the a's."

"Ain't no a's in it," said Rohwer. "It's R-o-l-f."

Williams gave him a hard look. "German, huh?"

"Now you're getting it."

"Lousy Hun," said Williams, curling his lip extravagantly.

"How did a nice guy like you ever get along with 25 sensitive ballplayers?" Rolf said, and laughed at the image. He asked if Ted had ever blown his stack during the season. "You know, really let go."

"Only once," Williams said. "Everybody in the lineup, seemed like, was striking out on high fastballs, and I was up to here with it. Then one day Casanova or somebody struck out on another high fastball—the kind of pitch you ought to really cream—and I just saw red. I had this bat I always carry on the bench, something to hold on to, and I swung it hard and, kerpow! I hit the bat rack. Broke two bats. I'll tell you, that shook 'em up a little."

He said he'd told the Senators from that first day at Pompano, "'I know you've heard a lot about what an impatient guy I'm supposed to be, but I think you'll find I'll have patience. The only thing I will absolutely insist on is that you hustle. I played this game 25 years, and it was always fun for me, fun to practice, to take extra hitting, even after a game, and that's the way I want it to be for you. So I expect you to hustle. I'll insist on that.'

"And they did. They hustled all year. And I wish you could have had a tape recorder on that bench, all the noise, all the clanging and banging."

He said when the team occasionally reverted to form and lost four or five games in a row, which it did several times, he made it a point to pay owner Short a visit. To "look him up when everybody was bitching and say, 'Gee, what a wonderful opportunity you've given me.'"

The safari was as good as over now. I left a couple days early,

His telephone calls—
"It's only me"—had
gone sour near the
end in Washington,
and by the time the
team was moved,
he had lost virtually
all enthusiasm
for the job.

having an assignment to tend to in New York (Ted didn't take it well when I told him I was pulling out; I don't think he relished the long trip home without someone to argue with). He finally packed his gear and headed down to Kariba Lake to go for tiger fish, which he said he handled with consummate ease, but it was an anticlimax. Then he, too, left Zambia, albeit with regrets.

Rolf Rohwer told me later Ted was already making plans to return. Rolf said he invited him to come in August or September, to beat the rains, the best months to hunt.

"No good," Ted told him. "That's the middle of the baseball season. But if I get a lot of aggravation, as I'm sure to get, and if we're not doing well, which is a distinct possibility, I'll just quit and catch the first plane out. I'd rather hunt than fool around with baseball anyway."

But Rolf said he smiled when he said it.

What, then, did that season amount to beyond the obvious? That for much of what he felt about baseball and what he contributed to its most important elements, Ted Williams had been vindicated. I would be tempted to say "fulfilled," but that wasn't there for him, not as a manager, not in the end. I doubt he really thought it would be. Managing was a toe in the water. A test drive with no real intention to buy. But I think you could certainly argue the case that for that one season, from first pitch to last, he was the happiest he had ever been in baseball, having proved himself once again while steering clear of the usual angst and controversy. He said as much several times in our conversations, without really saying it.

But the words from the friend on the yellow paper were correct. Managing a team in the big leagues was beyond Ted Williams' survival skills. His next three years were increasingly *un*fulfilling. The Senators went from not-so-good to bad-to-worse as Bob Short turned out (almost prophetically, considering) to be well short of the wherewithal to make the needed upgrades. Instead, he engaged in some bizarre trades, including one for the left side of his infield, and sacrificed potential to bring in fallen-star pitchers like Denny McLain, for whom Ted had no appreciation whatsoever.

The Washington team, as a result, reversed itself. In 1970, it won only 70 games and lost 92. In 1971, it plunged farther, to 63–96. By then Williams was wearied of the task. He admitted to me that he had turned almost hostile to some players, and bitingly sarcastic. He said he told a couple they ought to try another line of work. What *they* didn't know was that his last try at marriage was also failing. He and Dolores had separated, even with their second child, Claudia, on the way and the first, John-Henry, growing to an age where he could be a regular partner (albeit a small one) in Ted's outdoor adventures. The few times I saw Ted and Dolores together during that period were fraught with tension. They were on their way to a heated, bitter divorce.

In Texas, for that last season of managing, Ted was back living alone in a hotel room. I never saw him there, and, envisioning the sorrowful picture it presented, was glad not to. His telephone calls—"It's only me"—had gone sour near the end in Washington, and by the time the team was moved, he had lost virtually all enthusiasm for the job. He kept saying things like, "The Miramichi looks a helluva lot better to me than this." I was, in fact, surprised he stayed on for the move to Texas, but he made it sound as if he had a promise to keep with Bob Short. It was not a rewarded denouement. The Rangers lost 100 games, and finished dead last, and Ted crossed his name off the roster and went home to Islamorada, never again to return to baseball. His last stand.

But I think that brief shining moment of a first season had been a revelation. The "last of the .400 hitters," the man who set the bar so high that nobody has cleared it again in more than 60 years, had proven, in one small laboratory of application, that when it came to hitting, he was still in a league of his own.

For years after that, when asked about managing, Ted had an automatic, end-of-discussion response: "Boy, what a lousy job *that* was." The songwriter's lament that "a fool will lose tomorrow looking back for yesterdays" didn't apply. He was no fool. And I don't think he ever looked back with any real regret or wistfulness. He returned to his tackle box, and to answering the periodic requests for interviews about the mysteries of hitting .400.

But for that one golden interlude . . .

CHAPTER 5

Four Oh Six

I N 1941, JUST 23 YEARS OLD and in only his third year in the
major leagues, Ted Williams made the perfectly wonderful
mistake of hitting .406 for the Boston Red Sox. No one had
hit .400 or better for 11 years prior. No one has done it since—
63 years and counting. The .406 has taken on a distant aura, like
a planet; an accomplishment of almost unapproachable brilliance, as if it were done by Rembrandt instead of a skinny kid
from San Diego.

Rarely has a batter in either league made a run at .400 since
that .406. Williams himself came close in 1957 when, pushing
40, he hit .388. A much younger Rod Carew of the Minnesota
Twins equaled the .388 in 1977. George Brett of Kansas City hit
.390 in 1980, but no player in the American League has reached
even .380 in the intervening 24 years. In 1994, Tony Gwynn of
San Diego, a Williams disciple ("I read your book!" he said to Ted),
hit .394, but dropped from contention in the seasons after that.

Batting championships are routinely won with averages in the .350 range these days, sometimes well under that. Carl Yastremski won one with a .301.

> *The .406 has taken on a distant aura, like a planet; an accomplishment of almost unapproachable brilliance, as if it were done by Rembrandt instead of a skinny kid from San Diego.*

"Mistake" was Ted Williams' word to describe the .406, used sarcastically, for effect I'm sure, as the feat expanded in the public consciousness, and he felt the need every now and again to give the impression it was being over-examined. He knew better, of course. It was the central jewel in his crown, well worth examining, and as connected to his status as a man's hand is to his wrist.

As a latecomer to the phenomenon, I was surprised by how often the ".400 thing" kept coming up in Ted's presence, kept getting insinuated into conversations and situations. Senator Bob Graham mentioned it quite out of the blue while we were visiting in his Tallahassee office when he was governor of Florida—just laid it out as a passing tribute. In a doubles match one day at the tennis club where we sometimes played in Miami, Ted called out "four-oh" when he and I went ahead by that score, and one of our opponents yelled back, as if to complete the sentence, "Four-oh-*six*!" Ted growled, "Yeah, yeah, yeah."

At a fishing camp on the Parismina River in Costa Rica, where we had gone for snook and tarpon, I was in a poker game with three other unwinding fishermen when one of them, also without preamble, asked Williams if he thought anybody in the big leagues would ever hit .400 again. Ted, no poker player, was in a nearby chair reading a sportsman's magazine. "I sure hope so," he said without looking up. "I'd hate to think I'm gonna have to answer that question the rest of my life."

It was his stock reply to a stock question. And I heard it often enough to think he truly was tired of the fuss; that the .406 really was a mistake for what it had done to his precious privacy. But I came to realize quite the opposite, and to better see how much it meant to him and to his stated desire from childhood ("I wished it on every falling star") to be "the greatest hitter who ever lived." Because the "greatest hitter" designation would always be unverifiable, like calling Steinbeck America's "greatest writer." The .406 was—is—an indelible mark in the record book, and I began to appreciate the depth of his feelings for it when Rod Carew was bearing down.

It was, of course, that time of year: late summer, early fall, when the pennant races were in overdrive (and the salmon, too, in the waters of the Miramichi) and the occasional pretender to the throne got close enough to inspire the media to seek Williams out. Ted could always be found at his camp on the Miramichi then, going for his favorite fish, which meant he wasn't likely to answer the phone. This time no call was necessary. I was there to fish with him, and to weed out for publication his thoughts on the subject.

And he said pretty much what I expected. That he would "love to see Carew hit .400, for a lot of reasons—number one being I won't have to answer any more questions about whether it can be done or not and I can fish the baseball seasons in peace, stay right here in New Brunswick and not fly around getting my picture taken with any more potential .400 hitters." Besides, he said, he'd been predicting for more than 30 years that he thought it could be done, "and I'd like to be proved right for a change."

He seemed genuinely pleased that it might be done by Rod Carew—"a damn good hitter, and a deserving one." He said when he first saw Carew in the late sixties he didn't think he had the talent. "He was a little too lackadaisical to suit me. He swung at bad balls, and he didn't make contact that much. He still *looks* lackadaisical, but that's his style. He's so smooth he seems to do it without trying. Some guys—Pete Rose for one, and I put myself in that category—have to snort and fume to get everything going. Carew doesn't."

He said when he met Carew face-to-face that year, he marveled at what a specimen he was. "A picture-book athlete. Handsome and smooth-skinned, and built like an Olympic track star. Not great size, but a lithe, powerful, molded-looking body, and sprinter's legs. I remember how I envied the way he could run, how he seemed to fly without lifting his legs." He said he had asked Carew, then 31, if he'd lost any of his speed, and Carew said, "'Yeah, Ted, about a half a step.' And I thought, oh, baby, I'd still take it. If I'd had his speed, I think I'd have averaged .370." (Williams' lifetime average was .344; none of today's major leaguers come close to that.)

He referenced once more the 1957 season, when at .388 he was within five hits of hitting .400 again. "What's five hits?" he said. "I was 39 years old, aging and aching. There had to be at least five leg hits for a younger Ted Williams." But, he conceded, even a younger Williams was no Rod Carew going down the line. "Counting bunts, Carew will get 40 infield hits a year. The most I could hope for was 10 or 12. It's a big factor. Hey, with his speed I think Carew could *bunt* .400 if he wanted to." Of course, he said, they were opposites in that regard. Carew was "a singles hitter, and I don't downgrade him when I say that. It's simply the case. He's had years when he only hit two or three home runs, and one when he didn't hit any. Of the hits he gets, less than 25 percent go for extra bases."

> *The .406 was— is—an indelible mark in the record book, and I began to appreciate the depth of his feelings for it when Rod Carew was bearing down.*

Yes, Williams said, it was to his advantage overall that he had been a long-ball hitter. "But you don't have to hit boomers to hit .400. There are more important factors. For one, if you've got the kind of speed [Rod Carew] has, infields have to close in on you, especially at third. When they do, hitting angles quickly widen out. Infielders don't have the time to cover their territory and a hard-hit ball—and some not so hard-hit—gets through. I *know* the difference a drawn-in infield makes because I seldom saw one. The infielders always played me deep. Nobody feared my speed.

"But this is the big thing, for any hitter you care to mention, in any era: that you don't fluke into a .400 season. Period. A lot of guys have lucked into .300, it happens all the time. But there are no flash-in-the-pan .400s."

He had asked Carew, then 31, if he'd lost any of his speed, and Carew said, "Yeah, Ted, about a half a step.' And I thought, oh, baby, I'd still take it. If I'd had his speed, I think I'd have averaged .370."

There were, however, "circumstances," he said. "Good hitting runs in cycles, rising or falling with the quality of the pitching. In 1941, there were a lot of name pitchers in the American League, but most of them were over the crest. There was some great hitting that year. DiMaggio hit safely in 56 straight games. A guy you never heard of, Cecil Travis, hit .359. It was one of those years." But the fact was, he said, hitting .400 today "should be a lot easier than it was in 1941, and it doesn't take a Boston writer to see the reasons why."

He said for years the big leagues had been instituting ways to help the hitters. Lowering the pitcher's mound was a big one, giving pitchers less thrust and leverage coming off the mound with their throws. And reducing the dimensions of the strike zone, at least for practical purposes ("they *never* call the letter-high fastball a strike anymore"). But most important, he said, "they've expanded the leagues three times since I retired as a player in 1960. Just about every big city in the country has a team. And the record of every good player in baseball should be helped by expansion, that and the decline of the minor leagues."

He said you couldn't escape the mathematics. There were simply fewer good pitchers pitching in professional baseball, and with *more* of them in the big leagues—50 or so starting who would be in the minors were it not for expansion—the hitter had a much greater advantage.

What struck me each time I heard these arguments was that Williams was never inconsistent with his evaluations. It was like a mantra. And while he protested being "tired" of talking about it, I noticed that it never stopped him from, well, talking about it. Usually in amazing detail—naming names, places, circumstances, etc.—and with an animation that exposed the depth of his convictions. The passion for hitting never left him; the batting cage and batter's box never stopped being beguiling places, the wellsprings of his expression.

> *The passion for hitting never left him; the batting cage and batter's box never stopped being beguiling places, the wellsprings of his expression.*

Off Islamorada, I have held on as he perilously rocked his bonefishing skiff while standing to demonstrate the proper way to hit a low outside pitch: "Hell, you can't pick your nose on this pitch. . . . You've got to be quick, be quick with the bat." In Costa Rica, he leaped from a circle of fisherman on the edge of a jungle one afternoon to heft an imaginary bat and hit towering imaginary home runs. "See that?" he announced. "It's an *up*swing, not a downswing or a level swing. They've been getting that wrong for years, the so-called batting experts."

And when his .406 season came up in a relaxed enough setting, he would talk about it freely, examining each facet like a jeweler. His accounts then would invariably include "the most thrilling hit of my career," the home run he hit that won the All-Star Game that year. Two on, two out in the bottom of the ninth, the American League trailing by two runs, a full house at Detroit's Briggs Stadium, and he hit a Claude Passeau fastball over the right-field parapet to win it. Film clips of him bounding around the bases, clapping his hands like a schoolboy and laughing unashamed, are a staple of baseball archival films.

Two on, two out in the bottom of the ninth, the American League trailing by two runs, a full house at Detroit's Briggs Stadium, and he hit a Claude Passeau fastball over the right field parapet to win it.

So with time and a more congenial exposure, I came to think of his camp on the Miramichi as the place where you went in the late summer to talk about hitting .400, or about hitting in general. Actually, to talk about two things: hitting baseballs and reaffirming his conviction that the Atlantic Salmon "is the greatest game fish God ever put on the planet." There was really no separating the two. They always seemed to dovetail. Ted had, in fact, committed to the Miramichi right after he won his last American League batting championship in 1958, a steal at .328 (considering his .388 from the year before). Immediately after the last game, he flew to Bangor, Maine, and drove straight through to be on the river the next afternoon, beating the close of the salmon season by two hours.

"It was cold as hell, and the wind was ripping down the river," Ted told me years later about that day. "But I'd been tying flies all summer and I had a yellow butt on a double-8 with a short shank, and I laid it out there. And I kept laying it out there—picking up slowly, laying it out. Then there was a big boil, and I put it out again, and there was that beautiful roll and the feel of weight that you get when he's taken the fly. *Whoosh.* He was way downriver before he jumped, and I could see him for the first time. Then he came back *up*river and greyhounded right past me. He fought like hell for about 30 minutes. A 20-pound hookbill. The best I ever got on the Miramichi."

Hitting .400 today "should be a lot easier than it was in 1941, and it doesn't take a Boston writer to see the reasons why."

On a visit some years after I'd been there for the Carew "evaluation," I arrived late and hadn't had a chance to talk to Ted except to exchange waves from the porch. He was on the other side of the river, in a canoe, getting into position to fish. I had unloaded my car and was in the basement, suffering a communications gap with the long-distance operator, when I heard Edna Curtis, Ted's housekeeper, scream.

Actually, it wasn't so much a scream as it was a shrill relaying of information from her vantage point (I imagined correctly) near the window overlooking the river. I'd seen her there often, looking out, never farther than a broom handle's length or two from her beloved skillets and double boilers. "Lord, God!" she called. "Come quick! Ted's in the water!"

I was in the basement because that's where Ted hid his only phone, on the bench where he tied his flies, sequestered among the mounds of animal hair, bird feathers, and tinsel that comprised the sartorial backbone of his creations. As a concession to the outside world, he would sometimes answer it there, but if he was upstairs preparing to fish or eat or sleep or make entries in his log, he was more likely to give it the indifference he thought it deserved. In the local directory, the phone was listed under "Spaulding Trappers Association," to further discourage intrusions.

He was a mound of wet leather and rubber and soaked-through flannel, and the water squished in his waders. His breath came in audible bursts and made cartoon balloons in the cold New Brunswick air.

I hung up on the operator and bounded up the steps to the main floor of the cabin. Edna was now on the porch, her apron to her mouth. I banged through the screen door but had to pull up short to allow my eyes to adjust to the late-afternoon glare off the Miramichi. Framed by the white birch trees that surround the camp, the great glittering ribbon dominated an altogether lovely view. It's hard to think of Ted Williams now without thinking of that view.

From the porch to the river it was a hundred feet almost straight down. When I finally saw him, Ted was already out of the deep water and trudging through the shallows, pulling the canoe behind him by the painter. In Rockwellian perspective, he looked like a large worn-out boy trailing home his sled after a day on the hills.

We waited for him.

"You don't look so hot," I said as he reached the knoll at the top of the crude steps that led up from the river.

"I'm all right," he said, wheezing.

He wasn't really all right. He was a mound of wet leather and rubber and soaked-through flannel, and the water squished in his waders. His breath came in audible bursts and made cartoon balloons in the cold New Brunswick air. He sat down heavily on the bench of the porch and began to remove his waders.

"Roy says you're a cow in a canoe," I said.

"There's a lot of jealousy around here," he said. "A lot of jealousy."

"What happened?"

"The water's high and I wanted to fish a spot on the other side. I was standing up, poling, and the pole got pinched against the middle of the current. All of a sudden I was over."

(I had a flash image of a grim scenario: the pole banging into his head, the canoe smothering him, his waders filling with water and tugging him down, the river rushing over him—CANOE FLIPS; HALL OF FAMER WASHED INTO OBLIVION.)

"You better get right in and take a warm bath and get some dry clothes on," Edna said, her practical jaw set. She looked at him sternly. "You'll catch your death."

"No time to shower. I'm going to change and go back," he said, and abruptly stood up and lumbered through the door. I watched the screen tremble in his wake and looked at Edna. She rolled her eyes.

"He'd do that?" I asked. "He'd go back now, cold as it is, after almost drowning?"

"It's still light, ain't it?" Edna said and went inside. She had, after all, said her piece.

Roy Curtis, Edna's husband and Ted's guide, arrived soon after that. He'd been off in the pickup on an errand and was back to fetch Edna home just as Ted retraced the steps to the river in dry clothes and waders. Told of the near catastrophe, Roy joined me on the porch to watch, both of us now jacketed against the evening's advance. The Curtises had been in Ted's employ since the late fifties. They bestowed on him a tender but cautious devotion, not so much on account of his celebrity, which they merely tolerated, but because of his uniqueness. He brought to their lives security in a wretchedly insecure world—a third of the citizens of New Brunswick were on relief in the winter—and the uneasy excitement parents feel in rearing a generous but temperamental prodigy. In turn, they ensured that all his needs on the river were taken care of. The porch where we stood was built by Roy; he had, in fact, helped build all three cabins in the camp. In the fishing season, he not only fished with Ted but also guided the visitors Ted favored with invitations to the camp. In the winter he made repairs.

Roy recalled the first time they'd fished together, in 1955, "when we were both young fellers." Roy was a stockily built man, sixtyish then, with cloudy blue eyes and cheeks that glowed like slabs of ham. In his taciturnity, he made the perfect companion for a fly fisherman. "He asked me if I knew anything about salmon fishing."

"What did you tell him?"

"I said, 'Some.' "

"He was pretty cocky, uh?"

"No. Well, yes. Maybe a little. But in 40 years on the river I've met an awful lot of fisherman, and most of 'em either they can't fish a'tall or after a year or so they start telling *you*. Most of 'em you have to straighten out for sure."

"You had to straighten Ted out?"

He grinned. "Some. But don't tell him I told you that. Thing is, I liked him right off. He's such a great big kid, you know. Just a dandy feller to be with. And, of course, now I really can't tell him anything. He likes to tell me."

"I think he believes he's the best at salmon fishing," I said. "Is he the best?"

"The best I've seen," said Roy Curtis. "Forty years, and I ain't seen none better, no."

He said Ted could "do it all," tie the best flies, rig 'em just right, cast to the toughest spots. "He can cover more water than anybody. He knows exactly how to play a fish, and he has a fine steady hand to release 'em, and that's an art, sure. Sometimes I just sit on the bank and never lift a finger. And *persistent*. Oh, my. He'll stay out there all day, any kind of weather. Stay and stay."

He nodded, and we watched from our perch. Ted was moving along the near side of the Miramichi, now a silver gash— casting, moving a step or two downriver, casting, moving. Edna brought us Scotch to warm the vigil. The silence between us grew as we watched. Then, when it was almost impossible to see, there was a small detonation on the surface of the water, a flash of tumbling flesh and a quick one-sided battle. The lone figure moved to the river's edge, his rod held high in one hand, his other reaching down as he bent over.

"He's releasing it?" I asked.

"Yeah," said Roy.

"All day for one fish, and he's releasing it?"

"Yeah," said Roy. "Persistent."

The next day, now dressed for the task, I joined Ted and Roy for the action. They'd decided to try Ted's leased pool at Grey Rapids, downriver toward New Castle. The pool there washes into a long stretch of rocky, active public water and makes a first-rate salmon run. By canoe, it was no more than two miles from Ted's camp, but it was a half-hour drive by truck. We circled back the 10 miles to the nearest town, Blackville, crossed over onto Route 8, and then picked our way down a series of unpaved side roads.

As we bounced along, Ted repeated again for me his reasons why the salmon was his favorite fish, just ahead of the two others that I was more familiar with: tarpon and bonefish. Of all the fish that swim, he said, he believed those three were worthiest of a sportsman's consistent attention. He had caught—and, for the most part, released—more than 1,000 of each. He usually fished for the tarpon and bonefish in the waters around his home in Islamorada.

"And they're great, those two, no doubt about it. The tarpon is a super fish, and the bonefish is a super fish. The tarpon is more spectacular—an eager fish that bends hooks and breaks lines. The salmon doesn't fight like that, but he fights. I've known a 12-pounder to run as far as any 12-pound bonefish, or jump as much as any tarpon, and take you a quarter mile downstream doing it. And then there's the other factors. Where you catch 'em, how you catch 'em, the skill involved. You catch salmon in beautiful surroundings, places you never get tired of going to. There's a constant expectation. You're always seeing fish, seeing 'em jump, seeing 'em roll, seeing 'em walk over a bar."

He grinned. "And there's the added pleasure of the salmon being extremely edible. Most game fish you can't eat at all. And *this* fish keeps getting on you more and more. You dream about it. You think about the next time, the ways you'll fish for it. The flies you'll use. If I only had one fish to fish for, it would be the Atlantic salmon. I'll be a little closer to death when I know I can't fish for 'em anymore."

Three men were already on the river, in the "public" portion down near a bend from Ted's pool, when we came through an opening in the shoreline bushes and reached the bank. Rigged and ready, Ted moved immediately into the public water, and I let him go so that I could be sure to fish well downstream and thereby avoid the scorn he would inevitably heap on my casts. The wind was angling into us, but it didn't bother Williams. He double-hauled to build up line speed and cast once, twice, and then a third time, with the line whistling out and the tippet rolling like a lizard's tongue to flick the water, delicately laying down the fly; a 70-foot cast, right where a zipper on the surface had signaled a fish.

Eventually, he moved around the bend to his own pool, and out of sight. But when I moved in that direction, following the conga line of casting privilege that fly fishermen adhere to on a river, I saw him hunched over near the shoreline, releasing a fish. I hadn't had a tug and he'd already caught one. It continued that way to lunch time, with no one save Williams having caught anything, and when we gathered at the bank for Edna's salmon salad sandwiches, Ted's presence drew a circle of fishermen, mainly to talk about weight and length of rods, efficacy of lures, and so forth. One of them, an older man in a baggy shirt, hefted Ted's rod and whistled. "That's a lot bigger rod than I use, Ted," he said. "Gotta be a weight lifter to use that damn rod."

"Eight and a half feet, that's all," said Ted, and got up to demonstrate, resting his sandwich on a backpack. He worked the rod easily, demonstrating.

"But you're a lot bigger than I am," the man in the baggy shirt said.

Ted gave him a look. "Yeah, and my eyesight's better, too, and all that other crap I'm supposed to have going for me. But what you really have to have out here is *talent*. That's what it takes. A little bit of *talent*." He grinned, then made a face as a younger man in a red hat and red suspenders, an American, lit a cigarette.

"There was some guy on the other side smoking when I was fishing upriver," Ted said, talking to the smoker but looking at the group. "I could smell it all the way across. I could *smell* it. I know guys who'd commit adultery before they'd smoke one of those damn things."

The smoker grinned sheepishly. The others laughed.

But Ted wasn't through, not when he still had a point to make. He said he had run into some of his World War II buddies at the Hall of Fame induction of Al Kaline, Duke Snider, and the late Tom Yawkey, his old Red Sox boss, and every one had quit smoking. He said that ought to be a lesson for everybody, "present company included."

We were done on the river and back at Ted's camp before dark. After lunch, he caught and released a 10-pound hen, closing out his allowable fishing for the day. I'd slipped on a rock working downstream and swamped my waders, but in my misery I'd chanced into a nine-pounder and landed it, and that warmed me some. Otherwise, the activity at Grey Rapids had been confined mostly to casting, and when the clouds thickened and the cold came on again, we went home.

Two men were waiting in the driveway when we rolled in, an old man with hair white as tissue and a middle-aged man with a big twitching smile that made you think bugs were loose under his skin. They identified themselves as devout Red Sox fans, a father-son team. The smiling man had a book for Ted to autograph.

Ted invited them to sit on the porch, and the white-haired man watched tentatively as the smiling man gushed over his hero.

"You could still play," the smiling man said to Williams.

"Play what? The piano?"

"No. I mean as a designated hitter," said the smiling man. "With those eyes, those wrists." He looked at me for approval. He couldn't stop grinning.

"Well, it takes more than eyes," said Ted.

"Oh, yes, I know. Yeah. I remember the way you gripped a bat. You always gave it that little extra twist before you hit. All that power."

"You remember that, eh?" Ted said, pleased. "Boy, one of my loyal fans."

The smiling man blushed happily, a baseball archaeologist on a hot streak, digging up remembrances. "And the milk shakes. You drank a lot of milk shakes," he said.

"Is that what caused the gut?" I asked.

Ted raised the side of his mouth at me. "Boy, down the totem pole you go," he said. "Right out of the top 10 of my list of friends. Maybe never to return."

"Bob Feller says you were the best," the smiling man said. "I read it in the paper. He says the days of the super hitters are over—DiMaggio, Williams, Musial, Mays. They don't make 'em like that no more."

Ted ignored the compliment. "Your dad's being awfully quiet," he said. "Must be a Mantle fan."

"No. Ruth and Gehrig," said the white-haired man softly.

"Well, at least somebody around here has some class," Ted said, giving me a look.

What did Ted think of George Brett? the smiling man asked.

"Great. I saw him two years ago, and I thought then that he

had it all going for him—great physique, great strength. And he's fearless at the plate. You'd be surprised how many so-called great hitters have more than a little fear up there."

"What makes Brett so good?"

"For one thing, he's not really sure what he's doing right, but he isn't letting it bother him. For another, he's hitting to all fields, which is something I didn't do for a long time. But it's still surprising to me they haven't figured out how to pitch him. They don't seem to attack any particular area, to try to get a pattern. The low outside pitch was the toughest for me. I got a lot of those."

"I said, 'Joe, when I played, I only had to worry about me. When we lose, my heart gets heavy and I eat a lot.' McCarthy said, 'Ted, you're lucky. I drank a lot.'"

"You think it's right, all the money they're paying some of these guys now?" the smiling man asked.

"A player should get whatever he can," said Ted.

The smiling man's father broke in to ask if Ted had ever wanted to manage the Red Sox.

"Absolutely not. Ab-so-*lute*-ly not," Ted said. He said managing was a pain in the ass. He said that when he managed the Senators he used to call Joe McCarthy for counsel. "I said, 'Joe, when I played, I only had to worry about me. This business of worrying about a whole team of players is for the birds. When we lose, my heart gets heavy and I eat a lot.' McCarthy said, 'Ted, you're lucky. I *drank* a lot.'"

The father and son laughed together.

When they left, I asked Ted if it was true he'd tried to buy into the Red Sox in 1979. He said no, but that over the years he "kind of thought I'd like to be involved" in one way or another. Not in a position of total authority, but not in a subservient one, either. He said Mrs. Yawkey had encouraged him to come around—she'd gotten him to escort her to her late husband's Hall of Fame induction—but he'd been reluctant because of those he felt were less than eager for his presence, most especially Dick O'Connell, the general manager, who was fired in 1977. With O'Connell gone, he said, the atmosphere was more salubrious, but what with his consulting work for Sears and the time he set aside for fishing and hunting, he didn't see much chance of becoming involved beyond the coaching of the young Boston hitters he did in the spring.

> "Joe Cronin offered to take me out of the lineup to preserve the .400. I told him if I couldn't hit .400 all the way, I didn't deserve it."

After dinner—during the preparation of which he gave Edna extensive advice—Ted turned on the radio to pick up the Red Sox game and then settled on a sofa in front of the Franklin stove to write in his log. Scrapbook size, the log was filled with daily episodes and details—water, weather, etc.—of his catches. On the first page he had written: "I start this book with 700-plus salmon, and feel I know one hell of a lot about them and may be (there's no doubt in my mind about this) one of the greatest salmon anglers."

A Reggie Jackson home run dampened his interest in the game, and he was about to repair to the basement to tie flies when I happened to mention Carew, and how the .400 barrier kept growing.

Ted said he thought for all those years there were "certainly players good enough to do it. Mays, for sure. And Clemente, with his great bat control. And Aaron. Kaline led the league at age 20, and I thought he had a chance. And Mantle, gee. Great power. Great speed. Could hit from either side. And playing on a Yankees team loaded with good hitters, which meant he got more opportunities. But Mantle missed the ball too much. Not quite enough finesse."

The bottom line, he said, was that so many of the all-time hitting greats from *any* era had not hit .400. Babe Ruth, Lou Gehrig, Joe DiMaggio, Stan Musial, and so forth. None of them did. And with the passing years, he said he began to think, at least privately, that maybe people were right, that it was too tough now, especially because he "wasn't seeing the devotion I thought was necessary to make a .400 hitter. Today ballplayers have a thousand distractions and too much time on their hands, and the money comes in a lot easier. In my case, nothing else mattered but the hitting. I lived to hit. A trip to the plate was an adventure—and a time to store up information, too."

He said that when the 1941 season came down to the end, and the possibility grew that he was going to do it, he felt all those things had factored in. And what made it so enjoyable, so rewarding, was that "so many people were pulling for me."

He said he remembered "going into Detroit, where Harry Heilmann was broadcasting the Tigers games, and Harry would take me aside and say, 'Now, Ted, forget about that short fence, just hit the ball where you want it, hit your pitch. *You can do it.*' Heilmann had hit .403 for the Tigers in 1923, and he was the opposing announcer. I have to laugh. The Yankees fans booed the hell out of Lefty Gomez that September when he walked me with the bases loaded after I had three straight hits."

He said one of the advantages he had going for him was playing half his games in Fenway Park, his home field in Boston. The right-field fence was "way out there, to be sure, and that was no advantage for a lefthander, but from any hitter's standpoint, Fenway's got that good, green background. Mr. Yawkey kept all the signs out, everything was green. And there were no shadows. And I had the short, high fence in *left* field that helped, too, not because I put many out there, I was a pull hitter to right, but because of another factor. I always said to myself, 'If you swing a little late it won't be the worst thing because there's that short fence, the defense isn't there, and any slices you hit can *still* go out.'"

He said the ".400 thing" got bigger as the year went on because "a lot of guys had hit .400 for two months and then tailed. And to be honest it got bigger for me with the years. I had to think then I wouldn't be the last to do it, or that I might even do it again myself."

He said "the only guy who tried to put me down [that season] was Al Simmons." Simmons, then coaching for the Philadelphia Athletics, confronted Ted in the Red Sox dugout tunnel one day near the end. Simmons had hit .390 one year for the A's, "and he was another big guy, except different from Heilmann. He had a swagger about him, the kind of guy who when somebody else was in the batting cage would say, 'Buy him a lunch, he's going to be in there all day.' Simmons wouldn't win any popularity contests.

"So I'm sitting there on the bench and Simmons says, 'How much do you want to bet you don't hit .400?' Just like that. I said, 'Nuts to you, Simmons. I'm not going to bet I'll hit .400. I wouldn't bet a nickel on it.'

"On the last day of the season, I was down to .3996, which, according to the way they do it, rounds out to an even .400. I'd slumped from a high of .436 on June 6, and in the last 10 days of the season my average dropped almost a point a day. It can slip away pretty fast if you start messing up.

"We had a doubleheader left in Philadelphia. The night before, Joe Cronin offered to take me out of the lineup to preserve the .400. I told him if I couldn't hit .400 all the way, I didn't deserve it. It hadn't meant much to me before. It meant something to me then."

That night after dinner, Ted called Johnny Orlando, the Red Sox clubhouse boy, "always a guy who was there when I needed him," and asked Johnny to join him for a walk.

"Johnny really didn't like walking as much as I did, so as we went along I'd wait outside whenever he wanted to duck into a bar for a quick one to keep his strength up. The way he told it, he made two stops for Scotch and I made two stops for ice cream, and we musta walked 10 miles through the streets of downtown Philly."

"Frankie Hayes, said, 'Ted, Mr. Mack told us if we let up on you, he'll run us out of baseball. I wish you luck, but we're pitching to you. We're not going to give you a thing.'"

It was a cold, miserable afternoon in Philadelphia for the doubleheader, but ten thousand people came out to see if Williams could do it. "As I came to bat the first time, the Athletics' catcher, Frankie Hayes, said, 'Ted, Mr. Mack [Connie Mack, the Athletics' owner and manager] told us if we let up on you, he'll run us out of baseball. I wish you luck, but we're pitching to you. We're not going to give you a thing.' Bill McGowan was the plate umpire. As I stepped up he called time and slowly walked around the plate, bent over, and began dusting it off. Without looking up, he said, 'To hit .400, a batter has to be loose. He has *got* to be loose.'"

Williams couldn't have been looser. First time up, he singled. Next time, a home run, then two more singles, and in the second game he hit a double off the loudspeaker horn in right center and another single. For the day he wound up 6 for 8. He said he celebrated afterward with a milk shake. During the winter, Connie Mack had to replace the horn.

And there was something else Ted Williams consistently described about the aftermath of that .400 season. Joe DiMaggio, not he, won the American League Most Valuable Player award in a close vote, but in all the times we talked about it, Ted never complained. He said you had to realize that "the Red Sox didn't win the pennant, the Yankees did. And the 56-game hitting streak was a tremendous thing. A great accomplishment. Besides, hitting .400 wasn't as much of a big frigging deal as it is today.

"Hell, I'd'a voted for DiMaggio myself."

The next day we fished at a place called Swinging Bridge, only there is no bridge there, only the remains of one—an abutment that helps form a small island at the bottom end of one of Ted's pools and another abutment on the other bank. Once, they supported the cables of a footbridge. A heavy ice storm knocked it out in 1970, and there had been no move to replace it. The pool, well upriver from Ted's main camp, had a gravel bar that made a kind of spinal column for the fish to pass over. It was Ted's favorite spot, good enough to have accounted, he estimated, for half the salmon he had caught on the Miramichi.

We were joined there by a fellow member of the Miramichi Salmon Association, a longtime friend from Bathurst, New Brunswick, named Alex Fakeshazy. Fakeshazy was a bearlike man with a clement personality whose fishing outfit wasn't complete without a "Save the Atlantic Salmon" button.

The weather had improved overnight, and Ted was in high spirits. He showed Fakeshazy a fly he'd tied the night before. "Oh, baby, *that* one will catch fish," Fakeshazy said. Ted grinned and, fingers flashing, deftly tied it to his leader. "I should have been a surgeon," he said.

The prevailing wind came downriver at Swinging Bridge. Ted cast high, letting it carry the payload. "See that?" he said. "An easy 80-foot cast."

I was on a nearby boulder, sitting it out for awhile, so he obliged me with a blow-by-blow, telling why he cast at the angle he did, how the water was acting, how the fly was swimming. He reeled in and cast again, and, as if in response, stitches began to appear on the water in front of him, evidence of salmon rolling.

Ted worked downriver, casting. I had turned toward shore to get my gear when I looked back and saw him walking toward the bank, his line taut.

"Geez," he said. "I got bottom."

The fish he'd hooked made a spectacular somersault cross river. Ted grinned.

He never wasted a motion. When the salmon jumped, he instinctively leaned to it. When it ran, he waited for the moment it tired, then deftly turned it. When he had it flopping in the shallows, Roy put the net under and hauled it out. A 15-pound hookbill. This one, Ted said, they'd have to take home for the pot.

"What do you think of Ted Williams?" Ted said as Roy lifted the catch from the net and held it up by the tail. Roy finished the kill and laid it under a blanket of river grass for safekeeping. Ted curled his finger and thumb and pressed them against his lips and sent a chorus of "The Marine Hymn" keening downriver.

CHAPTER 6

When Enough's Enough

THE CHANCE TO KILL A BIRD NEVER STRUCK ME as much of a test of he-manship. This undoubtedly carries over from childhood when, with a Red Ryder carbine, I was unlucky enough to put a BB into a sparrow that had intruded on my neighbor's backyard just as I was drawing a bead on a menacing tin can. In flight, a sparrow is an impossible target, a hotdog wrapper on the wind. In hand, on that warm summer afternoon, it was a pitiful lump of inedibility. I wasn't impressed with myself.

But like Ted Williams, I passed out of that stage rather quickly when the outdoors became such an important part of my life, and hunting and fishing along with it. In due course, we both came to the same conclusion, he as a young boy in San Diego, me much later in Miami (and in subsequent adventures with Ted, when he was always willing to indoctrinate me on the subject): that there's a lot of hypocrisy out there in the form of conservational purism. By the natural order of things, Ted liked to point out, birds and animals and fish die, often through one form of battery or another, and just as often to the benefit of human beings. Letting A&P do your killing for you doesn't make it any more noble.

And, of course, nature is much more ruthless with its own than the controlled incursions of man with his quick-killing instruments could ever be. I do not argue that point with my non-hunting friends—to each his own—but I am convinced of its accuracy. Once, on a crusted plain in Africa, I saw a lion take down a wildebeest, and the dire emanations from the victim as it faced the horror of being eaten alive has stayed with me. If I had been closer that day, I would have put a bullet in the lion (Ted said he would have shot the wildebeest, too, if camp meat was needed) without giving it a second thought.

The other side of that coin is that the hunters I have known or hunted with are much more conservation-minded—more "humane," if you will—than the average American male could even imagine himself being, and Ted Williams was about the most conservation-alert hunter-fisherman I've ever known. He *never* took more than his limit, of anything, at any time, at least not in my presence, and openly rebuked those who did. He never fished or hunted where he wasn't supposed to or in areas he wasn't licensed to. And much more often than not, his fishing "releases" and forbearance in shooting his "limits" far outnumbered the times he legitimately killed and kept anything, for the pot or otherwise.

As for any possible reluctance to hunt birds, we talked about it only once, and dismissed it out of hand. When we fished, of course, such considerations never came up (people don't get exercised so much about killing fish). When we finally hunted something with feathers on it instead of scales or skin, it was mentioned only as a side-of-the-mouth follow-through to his invitation to join him: "You shoot ducks, don't you?"

"Only when they don't shoot first."

"Well, prepare yourself, because I've got something for you."

And with that he invited me to Stuttgart, Arkansas, to hunt mallards in the late fall. A friend had offered up his cabin in "a choice location" for the weekend and Ted wanted somebody to help him appreciate it. When offered such an opportunity, I tried always to be consistent. I went. I'd never hunted the fabled hot spots of Arkansas, and Stuttgart was at the top of that list.

Except that on this particular hunt the hunting turned out to be the only downer. We didn't even get close to our limits, unless you count those on patience. On the first full day, a wintry one, with a high cloud cover, we arrived early and stuck it out in the blind until it was almost dark, waiting. Even with the cold, the conditions seemed ideal—close to perfect vision, a natural flyway, with water filtering through the shallow ponds around the pin oaks, making for good positioning of decoys and easy retrievals.

But by early afternoon I was miserable. I'm not very good at biding time in a blind when the cold is numbing you up so badly that conversation comes out sounding like Mel Blanc cartoon renderings of Elmer Fudd and Daffy Duck. Ted, on the other hand, was stoic and relaxed. He acted as if he could stay there for days without lifting a trigger finger and be perfectly content, the kind of calm he always demonstrated waiting for tarpon. His patience, in short, was maddening.

We didn't even get close to our limits, unless you count those on patience. We arrived early and stuck it out in the blind until it was almost dark, waiting.

Shifting on the portable seat, I remarked how ironic it was that he showed so much patience in a duck blind or at home plate but so little elsewhere. "With writers, for example," I said, "and wives."

He ignored the sarcasm and said I had missed the point. That if he showed restraint in these situations it was because he knew he had done everything right—come to the right place with the right ordnance or tackle, best lures, etc. When that was the case, he said, he could wait on a flat all afternoon for the first tailing bonefish or "a week in a blind for that one shot." He said part of it was being "properly equipped," the "pride of ownership" in the gun or the fishing rod, and knowing you're there at the best time of day or season. He said when everything was in line "it doesn't matter how much fish you catch or game you kill, it's the total experience that makes it so good."

He recalled, as a case in point, a time in Princeton, Minnesota, when he duck-hunted with a native and the two set up in stands across from one another on the lower half of a lake to wait for mallards. A couple hours later, he said he saw his friend the native gather up his decoys, row to shore, and take his boat and belongings home. A half hour after that, Ted's view was crowded with "a nice little flock of mallards," anxious to get down among his decoys. He shot his limit in no time and took the results home, and when he showed up, the native "couldn't believe it. Well, you might call that having great patience. I call it being willing to wait when I knew everything was right."

Yes, he said, the same applied to having the courage of your convictions in the batter's box, most especially when it came to waiting for a good pitch to hit, knowing that to swing at bad ones would only compound the problem,

> "*You swing at a pitch that's an inch off the plate, thrown by a good pitcher who knows what he's doing, and the next time he'll throw it two inches off. Then three. And before you know it, you're batting .250.*"

would only make more trouble for you down the road. "I used to get criticized for taking 'close' pitches, and accepting too many bases on balls by *taking* close pitches. But let me tell you something every hitter should have burned into his backside. You swing at a pitch that's an inch off the plate, thrown by a good pitcher who knows what he's doing, and the next time he'll throw it *two* inches off. Then three. And before you know it, you're batting .250.

"That's patience, sure, and it applies to things I do out here. But look how little patience I have for a horseshit cast or a bad maneuver in the boat . . . or no style . . . or no talent when somebody claims to have it . . . or when I see somebody hasn't taken care of his equipment. It's like a stab in the heart to see the rust or the neglect of a good rifle or a good shotgun or a good fishing rod." He paused. "Or to see somebody waste a shot, like you're about to do."

I had seen the duck flying into our line of fire but well overhead, and instinctively brought the shotgun to my shoulder. Ted was right, of course; it was foolhardy. The duck was flying so high I wasn't even sure it was a mallard, though I'd guess Ted knew. No matter the brand, I thought of it as a maverick, and worth at least considering for dinner. And when I pressed the 12-gauge to my cheek, I could hear, like accompanying flatulence, Ted smirk in disbelief. I fired what seemed like light years ahead along the apparent line of flight, and to my surprise, the duck shuddered markedly, did a ponderous mid-air flip, and spiraled gently down into the pond in front of us. It seemed like it took a month to reach the water.

"Geezus. No frigging way you hit that bird," Williams said. He stood up and pushed out of the blind. "Awright, awright, you stay here. You need the rest."

He splashed through the water, loud and emphatic in his waders, and retrieved the dead mallard, talking all the way. He was grinning as he brought it back to the blind. "Look, not a scratch on it!" he chirped, turning the duck to an angle that hid the perforations. "He was so shocked to see the damn pellets up that high that he had a heart attack!"

That was the extent of our hunting for the day, if you could call it that. Darkness provided us an out. When we got back to the cabin we changed clothes and unwound in silence (except for Ted's occasional jabs at my "circus shot"), pretty much muted by the day's events. He had a couple of very large porterhouse steaks sizzling on the grill—"that scrawny duck of yours wouldn't feed the cat"—when there was a knock on the door, somewhat of a surprise considering how far out we were.

Ted opened it to a tall, whip-lean, stoop-shouldered man with gray hair and a weathered face that fairly glowed with mischief.

"Bill!" Ted shouted.

And Bill shouted, "Ted!"

They embraced. And it went on that way for a minute or so—"Bill" this, "Ted" that—until Williams thought to introduce me to Bill Dickey, and Dickey thought to introduce us both to the younger, smaller man who came in behind him. I didn't catch the name of the latter, being appropriately taken aback by having a New York Yankees Hall-of-Fame catcher come to life in our midst, one who had played with Babe Ruth when he (Dickey) was young and against Ted Williams when he (again, Dickey) was near the end of his career.

> *Ted was stoic and relaxed. He acted as if he could stay there for days without lifting a trigger finger and be perfectly content. His patience, in short, was maddening.*

Ted invited them to stay for dinner—*demanded* they stay for dinner in such a robust way they couldn't have turned him down. And for a couple hours, the younger man and I didn't do much more than nod and laugh from our lesser stations at the table as Williams and Dickey discussed everything from the smoke factor in Yankee Stadium when the stands were full to Babe Ruth's "failings" as a human being. ("You had to love him either way," laughed Dickey, "but a lot of the time it wasn't easy.")

They talked about the changes in the game, some not so good, some very much for the better, "and some a lot healthier, too," Dickey said. For demonstration, he held up his right hand. It was, in appearances alone, a conversation piece. Every one of the five fingers was bent and gnarled so that together they looked like a bouquet of crullers. Dickey said it was the consequence of having them broken so many times during a period in baseball when the catchers' mitts were much smaller and catchers routinely had to position their free hand next to the gloved one as a kind of back-up when receiving pitches. And thus routinely got their fingers smashed by foul balls.

"Most of the time we kept right on playing until we could get treatment," Dickey said. "You had to in those days."

Ted grimaced. "I *never* wanted to be a catcher," he said. "Never, never."

"Well, now, of course, they have the bigger mitts that catch everything," Dickey said, "and you see catchers doing this—" He put his right hand, balled into a fist, behind his back. "They don't have to risk leaving it out in front any more, they tuck it back here."

The conversation turned to Williams' .406 season, notably as it pertained to the viewpoint of an opposing player, and Ted laughed at a memory. He said he could recite word-for-word the conversations Dickey would initiate when Ted came to the plate and Dickey was crouched behind it for the Yankees. "He was always yammering at me. He'd say, 'How much you weigh now, Kid? You look like you're gettin' fat.' And *whup*, there goes a strike. He'd have me thinking about what he was saying and a pitch would go by. 'You ever hit to left field, Ted? You're always pulling the ball.' *Whup*, strike two!"

Dickey laughed and nodded his head.

"He'd say, 'Did you think that was a ball, Ted?' And I'd take another one, real close, but this time it *wasn't* a strike, and he'd say, 'How the hell big *does* that ball look to you?'" Williams paused. "And that goddamn [Yogi] Berra was the same way after you left. You both were the same, always trying to get me distracted, always trying to get me going."

He held up his right hand. It was, in appearances alone, a conversation piece. Every one of the five fingers was bent and gnarled so that together they looked like a bouquet of crullers.

Dickey said he remembered one time when Ted "hit one right out of my glove. I thought it was already there, and his bat came around so fast I couldn't see it."

Ted said that was what he always tried to do, "be quick with the bat," so quick he could "wait until the last split second to swing."

"Yeah, and then to hit it out of the damn park," Dickey grinned. "Because that's what you did. Home run to right. I couldn't believe it."

It went on like that through dinner and into a relaxed post-script by an open fire, and when it was time for them to leave, Dickey thought to add a little about his young friend. He said he was doing public relations for the man's family, whose company had spread its retailing successes across the country. He said he would have some stock put aside if either of us wanted any. Ted asked what it would cost for x number of shares, and agreed to do it. Dickey said he'd get back to him with the details, and Ted asked if I wanted some of the action. I said I'd think about it.

A month later, Ted told me he had, indeed, bought the stock, and that it was already "doing great." The young man whose name we hadn't picked up on, he said, was a nephew of Sam Walton. The stock was Wal-Mart. Ted said he wound up buying five thousand shares. I, of course, bought none. *C'est la vie.*

Which, at first blush, tells you something predictable about how the Ted Williamses of sport benefit materially from offers thrown their way, in almost any setting; how in Ted's case he blithely went about his business being an icon and itinerant out-doorsman while others eagerly shoved opportunities under his nose to take advantage of, if he had the time. And it brings me to the point of recalling this episode, circuitous routing notwithstanding (consider it writer's privilege, my being a sucker for duck-in-the-sky stories).

In Williams' case, he had always given the impression that he might not *make* the time for such opportunities. Those who knew him close-up sounded correct when they said he was inept at marketing himself. Naïve, even. Movie-star handsome, awesomely charismatic in that bristling, lit-fuse kind of way, he could have endorsed his way to a staggering affluence. He just wouldn't be bothered.

Fred Corcoran, his only agent in the strict sense of the word, told me how this impacted their initial "arrangement." Corcoran was a giant in the business, with an impressive list of clients that included many top athletes, and ran in the glitziest of circles (Bing Crosby was in one; so was Joe Kennedy). He was introduced to Ted by a mutual friend as "someone who needs your help sorting through all the offers," and Corcoran said he liked Ted from the start. But that over the years he really hadn't done much to earn his pay ("for every ten chances we get, Ted turns down nine and a half").

> "Ted sad, 'Fine, 50 percent. Fifty-fifty.' I said, 'No, Ted. Not 50-50. I get 15 percent. You get 85.' 'Oh, OK.' Money was not paramount in his thinking."

In the way of illustrating Ted's fiscal innocence, Corcoran recalled: "When we were talking about my job as agent, I told him that his baseball contract with the Red Sox would be his alone, to negotiate as he saw fit and to take it all, whatever 'all' was. And that I'd negotiate the off-field stuff, the endorsements and commercial contracts and whatever deals I might get. For that I'd take 15 percent.

"Ted sad, 'Fine, 50 percent. Fifty-fifty.' I said, 'No, Ted. Not 50-50. I get *15* percent. You get 85.' 'Oh, OK.' He didn't know what agents got because it really didn't matter to him. Money was not paramount in his thinking."

But even on its face it would be shortsighted to conclude by this that Ted Williams didn't appreciate the value of a buck, or the ways to get enough of them to make it work for him, and not just by having the sense to buy "bargain" Ford station wagons and "bargain" Army-Navy Surplus tennis shoes. He had, in fact, always demonstrated a pawnbroker's sensitivity for his market value when it came to his needs. If he didn't know precisely what he was worth, he knew what he needed, when he needed it, and how best to act on that knowledge. I first encountered the serviceable side of this asset when we were dickering with book publishers through my agent to do Ted's life story. The initial offers easily turned my young head, but Ted waved them off. "Relax," he said, "they'll go higher." I didn't, but they did.

The thing was he simply refused to be bogged down worrying about "strategies" for improving his finances. His approach was laissez-faire: let it come to you. He told me himself about the times he'd been ushered into investments through this friend or that. He said that his very first "counselor," in fact, was "a guy who used to sit in the bleachers in right field at Fenway Park. He had a real bald head that got as brown as anything. He was an officer with the State Street Trust Company, and he got me started. When he died, his secretary carried on. She didn't know as much, but I got a little portfolio going. Yeah, yeah, yeah, I know. I should have a couple million dollars in the stock market now, but I don't because I just didn't pay that close attention."

When Fred Corcoran died in 1970, Williams didn't replace him. And why should he? He had that steady stream of successful people eager to cut him in just to be nearby—people, he said, "who are a helluva lot smarter than I am." It was a qualification he wielded like a hammer.

The result was as good as an endowment. Without trying, Williams accumulated a number of major assets: ownership in citrus groves, a handsome stock portfolio, various land deals in Florida and the far west, the fishing camp on the Miramichi, a long-running endorsement contact with Sears and, eventually, the homestead and its trappings at Citrus Hills, a deal put together by his late friend, Sam Tamposi.

> *A simple caveat was always understood: whatever the transaction, it must not interfere with his play time—his hunting and fishing.*

The opportunities were continually being thrust under his seemingly reluctant nose. He said no until he said yes. A simple caveat was always understood: whatever the transaction, it must not interfere with his play time—his hunting and fishing.

Over the years, he and I participated in several properties together, usually brought to me by Jeannie Baker, the ex-model who had started her own real estate company in Miami and remembered the evening with Ted at my house not for his spectacular cursing (he didn't; he was on his best behavior) but for a voice that shook the pictures on the walls. No baseball fan, Jeannie had to be educated on Ted's pedigree, and he seemed to

157

like it that she *wasn't* awed. (She said she just didn't think of Ted as awesome; that she thought of him more as "cute.") Our infrequent transactions were always simple enough. If I got something I thought we might benefit from, I called him, and since mine were deals I could afford, I didn't expect him to reciprocate. When a lawyer friend named Dick White presented me with a chance at some land in North Carolina that could be "turned over quickly," he hinted that Williams might join in. I asked Ted if he was interested. "Sure," he said. "Just let me know for how much and tell 'em to get me the paperwork." Typical.

But there was a downside to this trust that caught me unawares, even as it exposed *both* our failings in matters with which we weren't familiar, most especially having to do with the vagaries of making money outside your field, and more personally, how it can becloud a relationship. A couple deals that had nothing to do with land but more to do with the use of our talents (and, in Ted's case, his name), put us at odds for awhile.

One came about when we joined contractually in the formation of a group intending to produce instructional videos. Ted would be one of the focal points, his views on hitting baseballs being eminently marketable, and he liked the idea. Other big names in other sports signified their interest in serving as "experts," too, but the venture died aborning when the party who had agreed to muster the funding pulled out when he couldn't muster enough of it. It was, he pointed out, "a bad time in the financial markets for starting something like this." It was also a bad time financially—in both time and money—for those of us who were the principals. We thrashed around for several months after that, trying to find a way to make it work, but we didn't have the time, the expertise, or the wherewithal.

The second came gaudily wrapped in the form of an offer from two men in New England to make a movie of Williams' life story, using the book we had written as its core element. Again, we both agreed, and contracts were signed. If we should have known better, it was not because we were not forewarned. Bob Franzoni, one of Ted's longtime friends and benefactors, and by then a friend of mine, too, had strong ties to the entertainment world, including having a son, David, who was and still is a successful screenwriter. Franzoni was skeptical. "These guys don't have the background to make this movie," he said. "Be careful." We weren't. And they didn't.

Ted was, clearly, a ship out of water on things like that, and so was I, but when in both cases the ship floundered, I was more astonished by his staying so far removed from it all. He kept virtually incommunicado, as if he couldn't stand the bad news, or just didn't want to deal with it. In both cases, lawyers had to be brought in for resolution, and that didn't help, either. The result was a prolonged period of silence between us, not broken until Franzoni convinced us both through separate lobbying that we had gone too far.

But I have plowed you through all this (consider it the scenic route) to relate to something much more significant about Ted Williams, having to do not with those times when he was out of his element, but when his most deep-rooted convictions surfaced into actions that *weren't* ambivalent. In other words, the extraordinary things he did to be true to what he believed about himself, and in his feelings for the people who might be affected by those beliefs.

This, I think, was best exemplified by two episodes in his life that we talked about, both historically recognized as negatives (and one a complete downer that left him devastated) but out of which I came to appreciate him more—or, rather, to appreciate his *values* more. The fact that they both had to do with money is immaterial.

The first was in one of those oddly poignant moments that gain larger relevance long after the fact, like a battlefield heroic or a pivotal decision in a laboratory. On a winter day before his last season with the Red Sox, Williams walked unannounced into the office of the club's general manager and demanded a hefty pay—*cut*.

Occurring as it did away from the field of play, the episode went unexploited in headlines of the day. Now, of course, it would inspire large bold ones, if only to suggest that Williams had gone mad. We live, after all, in an era of inflated entitlements, when even mediocrities who fail to live up to their own meager promise ask for *more* money, not less. And get it. And there is no shame in them. But shame was at least partly accountable for Williams' actions that day, given his obsessive respect for the talent God had given him. In his mind, he *deserved* a cut. And of all the events that define his wondrously unique—and uniquely melancholy—career, this might very well be the one that defines him best for me.

Charity had nothing to do with it, of course. Williams himself would have admitted that he was no less greedy or ego-driven than the next guy. At $125,000, he was the highest-paid player of his time, and if that figure seems puny by today's ridiculous standards (and a bargain for the Red Sox by *any* standard), bear in mind that in 1960 a Cadillac sold for $5,000 and a box seat at Yankee Stadium could be had for $3.50.

But what he had was a respect for his talent that went well beyond the manifest money-hunger of the modern athlete. When he walked into General Manager Dick O'Connell's office at Fenway Park that day to discuss his final contract, he'd already made up his mind. O'Connell had the contract waiting on the desk: "Same as last year, Ted," he said. "One hundred twenty-five thousand dollars."

But 1959 had been nothing like the same for Williams. That spring he was sitting under the coconut trees behind his house at Islamorada with a bat in his hand, telling Louise Kaufman what he thought he'd do that season, how good he felt. "I got up and started swinging the bat, just swinging it like it was a fly swatter." And he said with one swing he got a little too aggressive and turned in such a way that he felt a "twinge." He said he "didn't realize it then, but I hurt my neck that day. I'm sure of it."

The realization came at training camp in Scottsdale, Arizona. It was cooler there than it had been in Florida, "actually cold at night, and right away my neck began to bother me. I couldn't bend my head. To turn my neck I had to turn my whole body." Even the most casual observer could see that his exquisite swing was restricted. Skipping spring games didn't help; rest didn't, either. The pain got worse. X-rays were taken, and Ted was sent ahead to Boston and checked into the Leahey Clinic for examination. The diagnosis was a pinched nerve. He wound up in traction for three weeks.

The result was that Williams suffered through an "ordinary" season for the first and only time in his 22 years in baseball. Two seasons before, his improbable (for a man pushing 40) .388 easily won him his sixth American League batting championship. He followed it up in 1958 with his seventh, hitting a more temporal .328. But in 1959, barely able to face the pitcher as he set up to hit, he wallowed through one slump after another to finish at .254, his only sub-.300 season as a big-leaguer.

The Boston press, ever eager to count him out, pronounced the obsequies. A concerned Tom Yawkey suggested that maybe it was time to think retirement, that he was "hurting this year and I don't want to see you hurt more." He said perhaps the old warrior ought to rest on his laurels and call it a career.

Williams said Yawkey's assessment "fried my ass." He said he wasn't going to rest on anything. It had nothing to do with age, he said. He was injured. But his purist's pride told him that .254 hitters didn't deserve $125,000 a year. He told O'Connell in his office that day to change the figures on his new contract. That he would play one more season, for $90,000. "I'd gotten the biggest raises any player ever had," he told me years later. "It was only right that I take the biggest cut."

Williams turned 42 that season. Cobb, Ruth, Hornsby, Foxx, and DiMaggio were all retired by that age. His neck still bothered him. He said he still didn't feel "swishy" at the plate. But on his first time up, in the first game of the season, he hit a 500-foot home run.

It turned out to be that kind of year. Aching and sore, he still managed to participate in 113 games, and was invited to play in his 17th and 18th All-Star Games ("out of the manager's kindness," he said). His average stayed above .300 all season and locked in at .316, not up to his heavenly standards, but only five points shy of still another batting championship. He hit 29 home runs—his last in his very last game on his very last turn at bat.

"It was a raw, gray, drizzly, doghouse day" at Fenway Park, he recalled, and the Red Sox team was the worst in years, but the little crowd of ten thousand reacted to his legendary blow "like nothing I've ever heard. They really put it on."

As he rounded the bases, he said he thought about tipping his cap. But he had vowed those many seasons before when he had felt so abused by their treatment that he would never acknowledge the Boston fans again. And he didn't—not, in fact, until decades later when, as an old man restricted by two strokes and gripping a walker, he grandly waved his cap for a final farewell. But back then, in 1960, he couldn't do it. "I was just fed up with that part of the act. But you couldn't imagine the warm feelings I had, having done what every ballplayer would want to do on his last time up, having wanted to do it so badly, and knowing how the fans really felt, how happy they were for me."

We discussed his decision to inflict that pay cut on himself several times, it having demonstrated, I posited in the way of needling him, Williams' standing as a hopeless anachronism. This would then invariably dovetail into the broader issue, growing with the years, of over-inflated salaries in *all* pro sport, and their damaging side effects.

As I write this, in fact, the world has been alerted to the record $18 million contract Roger Clemens signed with the Houston Astros—for just one year of pitching for that team. Clemens, himself a former Red Sox, won 18 games for Houston in the 2004 season. By the simple math, this said that the Astros decided that each of those victories was worth a million dollars. There is no way of knowing what Williams would say about *that*, of course, but the night on the Miramichi when his visitor had asked what he thought about "all that money they're paying some of these guys now," he'd said only that "a player should get whatever he can, while he can." Later, he felt the need to elaborate.

He said for "far too long the pendulum went the other way, with only a handful of the top guys getting anything." That the salary structure had been skewed against the players. But now, he said, it was "going too far the *other* way," and he capsulated what he thought was the crux of the problem, namely players being motivated more by money (and the status it brought by headlines that routinely compared contract figures) than by achievement. "I'm for the players, now and always, but the question I have is how a .280 hitter can justify his millions in the fans' eyes. Or in his own, for that matter. I asked for a pay cut my last year because I hadn't done a damn thing the year before. I couldn't justify the salary I was getting."

He said maybe the worst part was that free agency and all the money flowing from its exercise was turning big league players into "gypsies." That owners with the deepest pockets weren't bothering to develop players (or any semblance of fidelity to team) through farm systems anymore, "they just pile the dough in front of a guy and lure him away." He said the result was that you could no longer identify some of the game's biggest stars with a single team.

"How many teams has Reggie Jackson played for?" he asked

"I dunno. More than a couple," I said.

"Yeah, and when he makes the Hall of Fame, because he's a great player, and he will, which one will they say he represented?"

"Same answer."

I said my problem with it was that the name on the shirt should mean at least as much to the player as it does to the fans; that the "loyalty clubs are always asking for should work both ways. How can you expect a fan to come out and support you if you don't honor him with *your* loyalty."

"Damn right," Ted said. "*Damn right.* I was a Boston Red Sox. When they talked about trading me to the Yankees for DiMaggio, I thought, boy, I don't wanta play in Yankee Stadium, not with all that smoke, not even with that short right field fence, which was always tempting. But the big reason was I was a Red Sox, and despite all the hassles I had in Boston, that meant something to me. When they talked about trading me to Detroit for Hal Newhouser, I felt the same way."

> *"I asked for a pay cut my last year because I hadn't done a damn thing the year before. I couldn't justify the salary I was getting."*

I said I thought there was more to it. That paying players in any sport beyond what they deserved (whatever "deserved" might be) was creating an artificial divide between the super-affluent athlete and the traditional middle-income fan, one that grew with each new extravagance and added to the contentiousness demonstrated by various (and sometimes violent) incidents at the parks and arenas. To keep up with their payrolls, teams kept increasing the price of tickets, parking, concessions, and memorabilia to such absurd levels that whole segments of the population were being shut out. That lower income families, traditionally the bedrock of pro sports' fan base, couldn't afford the tickets anymore.

"Hell yes, I *know* that's wrong," Ted said. "The fans are the ones who are paying for this crap." He said he didn't think it possible to underestimate the importance of making the games affordable for everybody, most especially young people. "We used to have 'knot-hole gangs' at the stadiums, where whole sections were set aside for kids so that they could get in for the price of a shoeshine. They don't do that anymore, and it's wrong.

Because that's where the fan interest begins, with the kids. They're making a big mistake when they ace them out."

Such was his academic argument on behalf of accountability in sport. What Williams did that day in Dick O'Connell's office was much more than an argument, however. It was putting his appreciation for the significance of his place in the game on the line. Signifying by his actions what Ted Williams thought of Ted Williams. He did not announce his decision, or suggest he might do it. He just did it. It didn't matter to him what people would think. What mattered was what he thought of himself, not as others might determine it, but as he had determined it.

There was one other time that stands out in my mind as marking the strength of character Ted Williams brought to sport, and it, too, was done in private. And it came out of the one great disappointment—the greatest failure, if you will—of his baseball life. The 1946 World Series.

The particulars are painfully familiar to Boston fans. The 1946 Red Sox were one of the greatest teams ever to play the game. Loaded with returning World War II veterans and with big names at almost every position (Johnny Pesky, Bobby Doerr, Dom DiMaggio, Mike Higgins, Rudy York, Wally Moses, and great pitching with Tex Hughson, Boo Ferris, Mickey Harris, Joe Dobson), they got off to a breathtaking start, leading the league from the second day, and after two months had the pennant all but clinched. They won it by 12 games over the Tigers, the World Series champions the year before.

It was the kind of season, Ted said, "that just breeds overconfidence." The Sox in one span won 15 games in a row, and as a team batted .271. In the All-Star Game at Fenway Park, Williams hit two home runs and the American Leaguers beat the Nationals, 12–0.

Despite the introduction that year of the "Williams Shift" by Lou Boudreau of the Cleveland Indians (who moved every fielder but the shortstop to the right of second base to thwart the pull-hitting Williams), Ted batted .342 for the regular season, drove in 123 runs, and hit 38 home runs. When it was over, he was named the American League's Most Valuable Player.

But with the pennant clinched early, and the eventual National League champion St. Louis Cardinals forced into a playoff to secure their spot, the Red Sox agreed to three exhibition games against a team of all-stars from around the American League. They were played in Boston, in 30-degree temperatures. Fewer than two thousand people, mostly in overcoats, showed up for each game, and in the fifth inning of the first game Williams got hit in the elbow by a pitch from a left-hander named Mickey Haefner of Washington. "Right on the tip of my right elbow, and *whoosh*, it blew up like a balloon. Turned blue. Hurt like hell. I couldn't take batting practice for two days, and the Series was starting the day after that."

Williams said he never used the injury as an excuse, and the public didn't know about it at all at the time. "But I remember wishing we'd never played that lousy exhibition." On his first time at bat, in the first game in St. Louis, the Cardinals moved into a modified Williams Shift and employed it throughout the Series, but it wasn't really a factor. Williams' performance was already fated. Hurting and dispirited, he got only five hits the entire Series, all singles, one of them a bunt. The shift, he said, might have taken away another couple. He drove in only one run, in the fifth game, and scored two. Eight times he got up as the lead-off man in an inning.

Grantland Rice, the sportswriting legend, came to his room at the Chase

> *And when it came to the part he had played in the Red Sox' defeat, he didn't hesitate; in fact, he volunteered: "It was my fault," he said softly.*

Hotel the night before the seventh game in St. Louis, with the Series tied 3–3. "I was lying there in bed with the lights out, thinking about how badly I wanted to do well, and now with only one game to play, and I get the knock on the door." He said he always liked Grantland Rice, "one of the fairest writers I ever knew," and Rice was "just there to boost my morale, that's all."

Rice insisted he join him for dinner, and Ted suggested a little place he knew, and when they were finished eating he said he told Rice that he'd "give anything" if the Red Sox could win. "I said, 'It doesn't matter what I do, just as long as we win. Mr. Yawkey deserves it. He's spent a lot of money, waited a long time.'" So, of course, had Boston. The Red Sox hadn't won a World Series since 1918.

It was not to be. Williams hit two towering fly balls that traveled 400 feet or more, but both were caught. He popped out with the score tied in the eighth inning and the lead run on second base, and in the bottom of the inning, the Cardinals' Enos Slaughter scored all the way from first on a double and won the deciding game for St. Louis, 4–3.

Williams said when it was over he couldn't believe it. "I was so disgusted, so unhappy. Shell-shocked. And so disappointed in myself."

When he got back to the hotel to pack, he absently reached into his coat pocket and found 12 blocks of tickets he had purchased to give away. "I thought, Geez, what's next?" He went to the train that night still playing over in his mind all that happened, including having read in the papers before the final game a story that suggested he might be traded to the Tigers. "I'd been worrying about what *that* might mean, and now we've lost the Series."

He said he went into his little compartment on the train, "feeling so down," and "when I got in there and closed the door I just broke down and started crying."

And when he looked up, there was a crowd of people on the station platform outside, watching him through the window.

On our last trip to Hernando to see Ted before he died, my daughter Caroline took video of some of Ted's conversation, and later when I looked at it, I had to smile. He had, without going into detail, brought up the 1946 Series as an aside, remembering that the saddest part was he "never got another chance to play in one," which had thus compounded the disappointment over the years. And when it came to the part he had played in the Red Sox' defeat, he didn't hesitate; in fact, he volunteered: "It was my fault," he said softly.

But that's not the end of the story, either. When the beaten Red Sox got back to Boston and Ted collected his World Series cut, he passed on the whole thing to Johnny Orlando, the clubhouse boy who had "always been there for me when I was down."

I had checked with Orlando about that and other facets of their relationship when I talked to him for the book on Williams' life. He said, yes, it was all true—that he was the one who'd first called Ted "the Kid" in spring training way back when. And he was the one who had walked with him for hours in Philadelphia the night before Ted put the finishing touches on the .406 season. And, yes, Ted had given him his World Series check, all right. Thousands of dollars' worth. "Just signed it on the back and turned it over to me."

But the glow provided by an exceptional act of gratitude is not the only value drawn from this incident. Ted Williams was being generous to a dear friend, yes, but more important, he was being true to himself. He didn't want the money because *he felt he didn't deserve it.* Just as he felt he didn't deserve what had been offered him to play that final season. He just wouldn't have it.

Consistent, Ted Williams was. To the end. Consequences notwithstanding.

CHAPTER 7

Last Words and Testament

I N THE HISTORIC—AN APPROPRIATE ADJECTIVE if there ever was one—2004 World Series, the Boston Red Sox, demonstrating a resolve ordinarily associated with avenging angels, swept the St. Louis Cardinals, four games to none. It was the first Red Sox World Series success since 1918—about the time science had conceded that the world wasn't flat. In Heaven for the last game of the Series, I like to imagine Ted Williams cheering every pitch from his own special perch, a sky box that would have included the irrepressible Jonah, who knew about ups and downs and dramatic comebacks; doubting Thomas (well, of course); Tom Yawkey and Joe Cronin of Red Sox frustrations past; several former Marine pilots; a number of fishing guides; and the various Boston firemen whose lifestyle Williams once openly coveted when his frustrations with the hissing and booing in Fenway Park had peaked.

The Red Sox' overwhelming victory in the Series not only was sweet for long-deprived Red Sox fans, I think it most certainly served to help mitigate once and for all Ted Williams' place on the goat list at Fenway, it having lingered there all those years for his part in their loss (to St. Louis, fittingly) in the 1946 World Series. The Red Sox, and Boston in general, had done much in the intervening years to demonstrate their true feelings—naming things and places after him (a tunnel leading into the city, a ".406 Lounge" at the stadium, his name and number across its interior facing), feting him grandly when he was near the end, etc. Four days after his death on July 5, 2002, Major League Baseball honored him further by permanently fixing his name to the All-Star Game's Most Valuable Player trophy. But the "'46 Series thing," as Ted used to call it, was one of those flies in the ointment that wouldn't stop swimming around. The Sox' 2004 World Series victory was the best possible eradicative.

As for me, with no other way to produce such a scenario short of an epiphany, I enjoy dabbling on the image of Ted being Up There in a choice location, making his presence felt—initiating conversations, asking questions, demanding answers—because Up There wouldn't be quite the same without him. Those persisting critics who would reasonably contend that the Terrible Teddy they knew and loathed couldn't possibly have made it are free to conjure their own much warmer image. This is mine, and I'm sticking with it.

Only a few times do I remember discussing with Ted the realm of such a possibility, and it first came up as an epilogue, of sorts, at the tail end of his own description of the most harrowing

30 minutes of his life. When, in fact, he was very close to death, not in the quiet hospital bed that finally claimed him in Inverness, Florida, but on a screaming runway in Korea, with fire all around. The episode resurfaced on our last visit, when Ted told my son Josh of flying jet fighters in Korea and having to crash land his stricken plane. But it requires more than that to set it up, so bear with me.

Ted Williams missed the greater part of five baseball seasons—1943 through 1945 in World War II and 1952 and 1953 in the Korean War—serving his country as a pilot in the Marine Corps. In the history of professional sport, no American star athlete has sacrificed as much time from the heart of his career. Many have served in one war or another, but none in two, or for so long a period, and what made those years so significant was what it cost Williams in the record book. It doesn't take higher mathematics to see that he could have wound up with three or four best-evers in major league batting categories, from runs scored to runs batted in to bases on balls and so on (his .481 on-base percentage *was* best ever). And since those times lost occurred when he was close to or at his best, it isn't too great a reach to believe that he would have had an outside shot at Babe Ruth's career home run record of 714, as well.

In Heaven for the last game of the Series, I like to imagine Ted Williams cheering every pitch from his own special perch, a sky box that would have included the irrepressible Jonah, who knew about ups and downs and dramatic comebacks . . .

175

We went over those possibilities a number of times for the books we put together and, with his being as goal-oriented as he was, not without eliciting his regrets. He had been, and remained, critical of the "gutless politicians" who didn't stand up for him when he was recalled for combat in Korea (at the ripe old age of 33), their having taken a pass on legitimate opportunities to grant him a bye. But never once did he say he regretted serving in that war, or in World War II, either. And when he talked about his service, he routinely called flying for the Marines "the second best thing that ever happened to me." He said he had griped about going back at such a pivotal time in his career, "but I met guys over there who had three, four kids, and they weren't complaining, so how could I?"

> *In the history of professional sport, no American star athlete has sacrificed as much time from the heart of his career, and what made those years so significant was what it cost Williams in the record book.*

And he said something else in that context: "If I hadn't had baseball to come back to, I'd'a probably stayed on in the service as a Marine officer. I *know* I would have."

Plus, he said, he loved flying. "I always had a feel for speed, so the flying part came easy. From my earliest baseball days I'd have those new cars and I'd zip around the highways at 80 or 90 miles an hour, so it wasn't all that great a transition to flying airplanes. But I had a healthy respect for what it all meant, what being way up off the damn ground meant. I'd seen what could happen in jet crashes. One in particular, when I was in training at Willow Grove, Pennsylvania. The plane and the pilot were just *crunched*. So I was never a totally relaxed flyer, because I knew it was my ass if I didn't pay attention."

Williams originally trained as a fighter pilot in World War II propeller-driven aircraft and was in position for combat in the Pacific in 1945 when the Japanese surrendered. Then, in 1952 after the Korean War broke out, his reserve unit was called to active duty. Almost immediately he was in Korea, where

> *"If I hadn't had baseball to come back to, I'd'a probably stayed on in the service as a Marine officer. I know I would have."*

he wound up flying 39 combat missions. One of his wingmates there was John Glenn, the eventual astronaut, and they stayed in touch from then on, but "I loved all those guys. Smart, dedicated, gung-ho guys. I said it then and I'll say it now. The best team I ever played for."

Williams was assigned to the Third Marine Wing, 223rd Squadron, flying F-9 jets out of Pohang—"a doghouse of a base, cold and damp and awful; I slept on a cot made out of four-by-sixes and the inner tube from an old jet tire." After his eighth or ninth mission, he developed a bad head cold and chest congestion that dogged him for the rest of his tour ("I was going to the infirmary about every other day"), but it did not stop him from flying.

On the mission in question, his squadron was well past the 38th parallel into North Korea, zeroing in on a large troop concentration. But as he neared the target, Williams lost visual reference with the jet in front of him, "and when I swung out to pick him up and then came back in line, I was too low. We were supposed to be low, anyway, using anti-personnel bombs, what they call 'daisy-cutters' that hit and spread out, but at that altitude *I* was the target, for I don't know how many thousands of enemy troops were in that encampment. Sure as hell I got hit with small arms fire."

I enjoy dabbling on the image of Ted being Up There in a choice location. . . . Those persisting critics who would reasonably contend that the Terrible Teddy they knew and loathed couldn't possibly have made it are free to conjure their own much warmer image.

When he pulled up and out of his run, "all the red lights were on in the plane, and the damn thing started shaking. My stick stiffened up, so I knew I had a hydraulic leak. Fuel warning light, fire warning light—there are so damn many lights on a damn jet that when anything serious goes wrong the lights almost blind you."

He said he started calling right away to his accompanying jets and one came up behind him, flown by a young lieutenant named Larry Hawkins from Pine Grove, Pennsylvania. "[Hawkins] could see I was calling, nodding my head, and the last thing I heard was 'I can barely read your transmission,' and the radio pooped out." Williams didn't know it but his jet was leaking fuel, and there were the first signs of fire coming out. He said Hawkins told him later that he kept yelling over the radio for Ted to shoot the canopy and bail out, "and if I'd heard him and realized what was happening I probably would have."

Hawkins closed the gap between the two planes and came up on Ted's side, close enough to signal frantically that the wounded jet was leaking fuel. He then gestured with his thumb to "get up," and the two jets climbed, using altitude as a safety factor, the thinner air helping minimize the fire hazard. There was another advantage, Williams said. "When you're up high enough in an F-9, you can glide 35 or 40 miles if the engine fails."

"All the red lights were on in the plane, and the damn thing started shaking. Fuel warning light, fire warning light—there are so many lights on a jet that when anything serious goes wrong the lights almost blind you. I was in trouble."

Williams climbed to 18,000 feet, to where he could see an expanse of frozen water on his right, and prepared for the possibility of bailing out—removing his leg strap, going off the hydraulic system. He said he had always dreaded such a prospect. It was the one real fear he had flying jets, that if he had to bail out he wouldn't make it. "The cockpit is so small, and for a big guy cramped in like that, I thought I'd leave my kneecaps right in there." He said given that possibility he'd almost rather stay with the jet and take his chances. He was a ballplayer. Lose your knees and you don't have a baseball life.

From that point back to the field, flight time was only 15 minutes, "but it seemed like an hour." And when he got over the field, it was a madhouse—60 jets coming in at once from missions, all low on fuel. "But all I had eyes for was that little field. Then when I started to make my break on a fairly tight turn—*ffuuumph!*—a big explosion in the plane. One of the wheel doors had blown off. Now I had fire and smoke underneath, and why a wing didn't go was just an act of Christ. The plane was still together, and flying, but he knew it was bad. "All I could think of was getting on that deck."

He said he came in about 225 miles an hour, "twice as fast as you'd ordinarily do it. My approach was good and I'll never forget looking down at a little Korean village near the field." Seeing 30 feet of fire streaming from the plane, the villagers were "running like hell. I pulled the emergency wheel latch, but only one wheel dropped down. I hit flush and skidded up the runway, really fast. No dive brakes, no flaps, nothing to slow the plane." For more than a mile he skidded, ripping and tearing up runway, sparks flying. He said he could see the fire truck, and he pressed the brakes so damned hard he almost broke his ankle, "and all the time I'm screaming, '*When is this dirty son of a bitch going to stop?*'"

The jet continued sliding up the runway toward a second fire truck. The truck tried to get out of the way, dust flying behind it, and he finally stopped right in front of it, at the very end of the runway. The canopy wouldn't open at first, then he hit the emergency ejector, "and the fire was all around me. Everything on fire except the cockpit. Boy, I just *dove* out of that plane, and kind of somersaulted, and when I got up there were two Marines right there to help me." He looked back and the plane was spurting fire, and when he saw it later it was burnt to a crisp. "I mean totaled.

"I took my helmet and *slammed* it on the ground, I was so mad." He said he always screamed when he was mad and scared, and he was scared and mad sliding those last 2,000 feet. "And I musta yelled it two or three times going down that runway—'If there's a goddamn Christ, this is the time old Teddy Ballgame needs you.' Just like that."

There was a long pause in his account, and I thought he was moving on to something else when he said, "And I gotta say I think there is . . . I have to lean that way."

"You what?" I asked.

He said, "I have to feel that Christ is responsible for all this. . . . That somebody's gotta be in charge."

That was it. Nothing more. But I remember thinking at the time that he had said it as more than just an aside, or even as an involuntary spin-off from whatever remained in his thinking from having a mother who was so totally absorbed with Salvation Army service, but I didn't press it. We discussed the broader issue of God only once or twice after that, and then more in the way of Williams delving into *my* thinking than me into his (he being never one to leave a worthwhile subject unexamined). He said how he was "mad at God" a lot, and knew that he exhibited that anger in graphic terms with his language. My too-flippant response was, "That's OK. God can handle it."

When he asked me for specifics about my own beliefs, I had offered only the usual biblical emissions from a predominately Presbyterian background—and thought immediately that I'd either said too much or not enough. I suggested, since he'd "heard all that" from earlier exposures, that for a more current apologia he should try C. S. Lewis. "Besides," I said of Lewis, "if you don't get the logic, you'll still enjoy the writing." I have no idea if he took me up on the suggestion, but in the last quarter of his life he had Louise Kaufman living with him, and from what I knew of Louise, she was a pretty good source for knowledge and convictions on such fronts. Her long-suffering dedication to Williams would have required it.

Again, some background is in order. Louise Kaufman took residence on the Florida Keys in the early fifties while still married to a successful Philadelphian, big into metal containers, named Bob Kaufman. They had five children, and by then a failing marriage. Louise was living out the end of it when she moved into a palatial (for Islamorada) three-story house near the city yacht basin, and became a Keys fixture. She fell in love with the place. And with the fishing. And, ultimately, with Ted Williams.

Though a few years older, she was certainly Ted's "type." She was good-looking, smart, articulate, and fished so well and with such vigor that she once caught a world record tarpon in the women's division of competition. But when he became available after his divorce from Doris Soule, Williams, instead, married Lee Howard, a model from Chicago and a divorcée herself with two teenage children. Louise went to Paris to get over it, but kept her residence on the Keys. I got to know her post-Howard, when Ted was between marriages again, and she had come back in his life on a "more intimate" basis. But then came Dolores

Wettach, and Ted's appreciation for same, leading to Dolores' pregnancy. And one day when Ted was preparing to, as he put it, "make Dolores an honest woman," I got a call from Louise.

"You can't let him do it!" she said. She wasn't screaming; that wouldn't have been her style. But she might as well have been. "I've waited for him through two marriages. You've got to tell him he can't do this!"

I said, "Louise, you overrate my influence. I couldn't stop Ted from marrying her if I wanted to, and I'm not sure I'd want to. This is his call."

Louise sold her house and moved away from Islamorada for a time after that, but not far enough to miss the williwaws from Williams' eventual marriage breakdown with Dolores, who by then had given him a daughter, Claudia, to go with son John-Henry. And when Dolores moved out, back to the Keys and into Ted's life Louise came. Except this time for good, and for all the right reasons. She laughed when she told Donna and me later that Ted had "threatened to go to church" when she returned, partly in deference to her religious leanings and partly because Ted had come to appreciate as a kindred spirit the rector at the St. James the Fisherman Episcopal Church, where Louise was a regular at the 8:00 A.M. Sunday service.

Ted hadn't actually darkened that particular door, Louise said, but the priest frequently came to his. The priest's name was Father Sam Hale, a hearty, gregarious soul beloved by his Islamorada parishioners and valued by Louise as someone she could confide in. She said whenever he dropped by the house

Ted welcomed him with Bloody Marys and reopened debate over the best places to look and the best tackle to use for bonefish. "And they discussed other things, too," Louise said knowingly. She called it "a very nice rapport." She called it "the mountain coming to Muhammad."

Of course, Williams didn't go to that church or any other, not to my knowledge, and his often profane outpourings didn't seem to be diminished much by Louise's permanence in his life, though I have to say that the times Donna and I were with them it wasn't one-sided. Louise had a salty tongue herself, and could give pretty much as she took. But she knew where to draw the line in a social setting and tried to impose that limitation on Ted. He'd vent, and she'd shake her head and put her finger to her mouth in a shushing signal and say, "No, Ted, no," and usually he'd ignore her. But not always. She chuckled one night in Islamorada when we were there and he'd uttered one blaspheme too many that "Ted Williams *has* to be thinking about God a lot, all the times he uses His name."

I wouldn't presume to guess how strong Louise's convictions about her own faith were. I do know that she exhibited an inner strength in dealing with Ted that was almost saintly. He could, as I've said, be especially hard on people who risked being too close, and she was certainly in that range. At dinner a couple of times, Donna gave me looks when Ted said things to Louise that were patently hurtful—about her appearance (as they aged, he could see the girth she added but not his own), about her cooking, about anything and everything. I told him when the two women were out of the room after one outburst that he "oughta cool it," that it was beneath him to talk like that, and he nodded, got up, and went to the bathroom.

But if it appeared to some that Louise had opted for a kind of *de facto* servitude to maintain the relationship, I never saw it that way. Louise ("Lou" to her friends) was smart enough and just tough enough to be the perfect complement, the best mate possible for a Ted Williams. She was still with him and holding her own when he sold the Islamorada house and they moved to Citrus Hills, and was there *for* him when he had his first stroke. And when she died in 1993, he cried openly to me on the telephone—great, gasping sobs—when I called to commiserate. "I loved her, John," he said. "God, I loved her."

> *[W]hen she died in 1993, he cried openly to me on the telephone—great, gasping sobs— when I called to commiserate. "I loved her, John," he said. "God, I loved her."*

Things were written about how down Ted was on God during that period; how "bitter" he was. I prefer to believe it was his way of coping; when he needed to let loose on inexplicable hurt, God had always been a convenient target. I also believe Louise's influence on his thinking, together with what he had experienced from childhood, ultimately prevailed. In Leigh Montville's marvelously inclusive, almost encyclopedic book on Williams, he quotes one of the nurses who was with him at the Hernando house near the end—tending his needs, wheeling him around in his wheelchair, admiring his stories—as attesting to Ted's final embrace of his religious underpinnings. Virginia Hiley-Self, who, according to Montville, had "grown to love him through the months," said she prayed with Ted about it and that he knew "Christ was his savior." I was reminded when I read it of a fiery runway in Korea.

Since Ms. Hiley-Self was there for the benediction, she gets the last word. I have no way of knowing either way, of course, and make no attempt here to ascribe a piety to Ted Williams that didn't exist. But he was an intelligent man and it had always seemed to me that he was certainly, if not constantly, trying to fathom greater meaning in the things in life that affected him, and God would undoubtedly have qualified for that. Whichever way you take it, however, Ms. Hiley-Self's conclusion made infinitely better sense than the absurdity foisted on him *after* his death—the one that left a nation of his fans incensed by the image of him awaiting carnal deliverance in a frozen food locker in Scottsdale, Arizona, his head and body separated and immersed in liquid nitrogen. Cryonics was to be his savior, not Christ.

The latter debacle, courtesy of his son, John-Henry (now also dead, quite ironically, from an aggressive leukemia), succeeded in making a burlesque of Ted's passing. If that, too, strikes those who value his memory as tragic, it is good to be reminded that Ted wasn't around to experience the embarrassment himself. I knew, from a conversation he had with Donna that one of my children happened to videotape on our last visit, that he did *not* want to be "finished off" that way.

Which also needs some elaboration, and requires that we forage at last through the most melancholy part of this narrative, when so much of the final stages of Ted's life didn't seem to make any sense at all. But be assured that on the other side awaits an upbeat ending. At least from my perspective.

This hardest segment must necessarily center on Ted Williams' unfortunate only son, John-Henry Dussault Williams (Dussault was Dolores' contribution), who I first remember—and will remember always—as a positively beautiful little boy with wide eyes and a huge unaffected smile, his too-large pants askew on his hips and a fishing rod quivering in his hands. The rod was twice his height, and his father snugged up behind him, giving hands-on, affectionate instruction on how to cast. I say beautiful because he was twice blessed with such genes, Ted's and Dolores'. But, sadly, that portion of the father-son relationship was brief.

> *Ms. Hiley-Self's conclusion made infinitely better sense than the absurdity foisted on him after his death . . . the image of him awaiting carnal deliverance in a frozen food locker in Scottsdale, Arizona.*

Dolores was divorced from Ted when John-Henry was four, but she stuck it out in Islamorada, her children enrolled in a Christian school, until John-Henry was a fourth-grader. I saw Ted only on occasion during that period and didn't see Dolores at all. She then moved them back to her home in Vermont to raise John-Henry and Claudia solo. There were summertime visits to Florida, and trips to the Miramichi, and Ted was there for his various graduations, but John-Henry did not reenter Ted's life to any degree of permanence until Louise was gone from it and Ted needed him.

By then John-Henry was in his mid-twenties, and into making his own mark—via his father's honored name. He had, in fact, with Ted's blessing, already started trading on it in New England with a company he started right out of college, Grand Slam Marketing. But he was clearly not very good at it, nor was he even close to realizing a grander ambition: to be a major league baseball player like his old man. Ted told me early on that it was a reach. He'd seen John-Henry at the plate, and tried to help, "but it'll never happen." John-Henry had been just an average player as a teen and through college, and when he decided to try again long after it was prudent to do so, got cut routinely from the minor league teams he contracted with. He was still embarrassing himself with unsuccessful stabs at the game when he was into his thirties and exhibiting the first signs of his fatal illness.

But besides a rather breathtaking unwillingness to accept reality, what was all that except an obsession with proving himself worthy of being Ted Williams' son (after all those years of perceived neglect)? Add to it the corroborations of what happened in the last stages: John-Henry's outrageous—and heavily chronicled—exploitations of Ted Williams and the Williams signature and assets, from the time he moved in at Citrus Hills until Ted died (excuse me, until *after* Ted died). Dolores told me once when it was clear they weren't going to make it that "Ted Williams hasn't seen the last of me." No shrinking violet, it would have been inconsistent for her to go quietly, or not to have passed on the sense of injury to her children. It is therefore easy to conclude that all of this was justified in John-Henry's mind. He was getting only what he deserved. A deferred compensation.

But look at it another way. The fact that John-Henry was willing to turn his life over to his father for those final years— even to the point of taking showers with the enfeebled Williams to keep him from falling after his last stroke—was certainly worth something. Did he exploit Ted Williams? Yes. Did he drive expensive cars—Porsches, BMWs—and flaunt all the usual suspects of conspicuous consumption? Yes. Did he make questionable, erratic business decisions in an ever-expanding search for enrichment, and turn Ted's name into a series of negative newspaper headlines, and Ted himself into a virtual autograph machine? Yes, yes, and yes. But for most of that time—until the last two years or so of his life, actually—Ted was functioning well for someone his age and all he'd gone through, still very much his own man and, being Ted, simply would not have done what he did not want to do.

It was Williams, in fact, who had already laid the groundwork for the "Hitters Museum" on land at Citrus Hills donated by his old pal Sam Tamposi. He had passed into a new phase, one that appeared to compromise his cherished credo of never *ever* allowing money to get in the way of his fun. Being so far removed from what was happening (Hernando might as well have been

Paris for as often as I got there), I was nevertheless surprised, for a very simple reason: Ted didn't need more money—actually he needed *less*, given the limitations age imposes—for the lifestyle he treasured. That had apparently changed. But how?

Chaos can have gentle beginnings. When Williams and Louise first moved to Hernando it all seemed to fit. With Islamorada over-crowding and the fishing not as good, and Sam Tamposi beckoning, they figured it was time to pull out. But if Ted had reached retirement age, he had no intention of hunkering down. He returned to the Keys regularly to fish, usually with a new favorite guide named Gary Ellis (Jack Brothers was dead, so was Jimmy Albright), and annually he made it back to his camp on the Miramichi for the salmon season. And when he was not fishing or hunting or hacking at one kind of ball or another, he could be found on display at the Citrus Hills development he had agreed to shill for, from his signature house on the golf course.

Joe DiMaggio and Muhammad Ali were among the attending dignitaries when the Ted Williams Museum opened to glittering reviews in early 1994, the year after Louise's death. John-Henry moved in at the end of that year, and as their months together became years, Ted embraced his son's presence—and modus operandi. His horizons necessarily expanded. So did his resources. At select occasions and locales—mainly memorabilia and baseball card shows, orchestrated by John-Henry—he could be found trading on his name. Bob Franzoni, our mutual friend and one of Ted's fishing buddies and business advisers from way back, said

Ted was "making more money in a weekend of autographing than he did swinging a bat all season as a young player."

If the image of the last of the .400 hitters signing his name for cash seemed out of sync as some contended, especially seeing as how Ted Williams had always been so generous with his autographs, Williams could have reminded them that an obscure modern-day major leaguer named Otis Nixon doubled his salary one year on the strength of a .217 season; and another named Cory Snyder more than doubled his after hitting .215. And never mind the millions upon millions the "superstars" were raking in. When I questioned him about it, Ted laughed and said he was "only making up for lost time." He called it "making ends meet—and giving John-Henry something to do with his life."

To be sure, the escalating controversies eventually bothered him, with his one son flitting around the country conspicuously and pugnaciously challenging (and sometimes suing) memorabilia peddlers over the authenticity of Ted's autographs. But it didn't bother him enough. I suggested once during a phone conversation after criticism of one of John-Henry's didoes had made the national news that if his son wasn't careful he was going to have the whole world doubting *every* Ted Williams autograph. "Yeah, he's a pain in the ass," Williams said. "But I love him."

Dolores came back into Ted's life as a sometimes house guest when John-Henry took over, but from all accounts their ability to find peaceful common ground hadn't improved. Those who witnessed their high-tension attempts said, "she hasn't changed, and, of course, neither has he." Ted told me he and Dolores "still can't last in a room for 30 minutes without fighting over something." I remember thinking how wrong my impressions must have been from years before, believing as I did that they were ideally suited.

On my first visit to Citrus Hills after his entrenchment, John-Henry, now a strikingly handsome man and taller than his father, was unfailingly polite and accommodating, and clearly in acquiescence with Ted's bullying style. To be sure, the bullying was affectionately applied, but there was no doubt who was in charge. John-Henry was sporting a girlfriend then whom Ted obviously approved of and predicted (incorrectly) that he would marry. "He *should* marry her," Ted said when they'd left the house and we were having lunch. "I *want* him to." So much for Ted Williams the matchmaker. But what was more assuring for me were the people who were providing the care he was getting, at the time when he didn't need all that much and later after his second stroke, when he needed a lot.

I'd met, at the house and a few times by phone, George Carter, an ex-Marine ("Is it any wonder why I like this guy?" Ted said) who was serving as one of Williams' live-in male nurses. You could not be unimpressed with George Carter. And serving with him was Jack Brothers' son Frankie, up from Islamorada. Having known Jack was enough to make me feel good about Frankie. The two, Carter and Brothers, were there for Ted through all the subsequent setbacks and procedures, and well into his decline, and would be on hand at the hospital in

San Diego following his open heart surgery in 2001—at which point John-Henry abruptly fired them. The assumption all around was they had gotten too used to doing what *Ted* wanted, not what John-Henry wanted.

But that was nearer the end of the disintegration. On the visit in question, Ted asked me to "get involved" with his efforts— his "campaign," he called it—to clear the name of "Shoeless" Joe Jackson and get it placed where it belonged, in the Baseball Hall of Fame. Ted was a big admirer of Joe Jackson's swing, which he had seen in film clips after meeting Jackson "way back when I first came to Boston." He called it "one of the prettiest swings I ever saw." Jackson was banned from baseball after the Black Sox scandal of 1919, when he and other members of the Chicago White Sox team were charged with throwing the World Series. His guilt was never established (Jackson was, in fact, a hitting star of that series) and Williams eventually decided that the penalty was a travesty. He said as his "final contribution to base-ball" he wanted to clear Joe Jackson's name. He said he had gotten George Steinbrenner to join in.

Buzz Hamon was the curator of the Williams museum then and ran interference. Hamon called me several times after that, saying that Ted wanted to expand the idea and maybe have me write a book about his last twenty years. Hamon said it was "something Ted keeps bringing up." When Ted and I talked, he said yes, he felt he still had "a lot to say." Both campaigns died with him. Hamon, by then gone from Hernando and what he called "the mess John-Henry's making there," eventually added his voice to the growing chorus of critics inveighing against John-Henry's actions.

But though I liked him, I didn't really know Buzz Hamon. I'd met him only by phone. It was the people I *did* know, close friends of Ted's from long standing, who made me realize how bad it had gotten. The craziness and paranoia that marked John-Henry's actions as the facilitator of Ted's new fiscal outreach had morphed into an almost systematic isolation of Ted's time and access. To my knowledge, my occasional calls were never deflected, my visits never discouraged. But he had certainly done it to others, and it didn't sit well with those who had for so long been so close (and, indeed, so valuable).

Joe Lindia I knew. A husky, chronically friendly man with a broad face that was barely broad enough to contain his smiles, Joe had been a friend of Williams from Ted's playing days. He was a restaurateur in Cranston, Rhode Island, when they met, and with his wife, Dottie, actually closed down his restaurant and moved to Florida when Ted asked him to join him at Citrus Hills. There, for a time, he virtually became Ted's driver. Lindia told me once that he treasured every memory he had of their times together, including having had Ted surprise him with an introduction to Ty Cobb. But with the passing years, "things happened," Dottie said, and it got "more and more difficult to communicate." Joe complained to me about the freeze-out twice before he died, the last time bitterly. Dottie said he was "heartbroken."

Bob Franzoni was equally offended. A highly successful Vermont businessman and marketer, Franzoni was one of those valuable insiders whose serendipitous offerings Ted profited by. He was a regular at Ted's camp on the Miramichi, and Ted just as regularly visited the Franzonis' home in Rutland and their cottage on Lake Bomoseen in west-central Vermont. But in the last years it became more and more difficult to connect, and Franzoni wondered if it wasn't because of the "discovery" he had made one night on the Miramichi, on one of the last occasions Ted had fished there.

Franzoni called me about it after he got back to Vermont. He said John-Henry had been at the camp, "although he never really seemed to like fishing with Ted all that much." After dinner Franzoni went down to the basement to use the telephone and found John-Henry "practicing Ted's signature on a legal pad. Copying from an original. One 'Ted Williams' after another. I didn't make a fuss, but he had to know what I was thinking."

I told Bob at the time that I thought he could have taken what he saw another way: that it might just as well have been *Ted*'s idea, as a way of relieving himself of some of the demands John-Henry had imposed with all that autographing. "Busy people frequently get somebody else to sign their names, a secretary or somebody. Politicians use a stamp," I said, adding offhandedly that I never could fathom the value collectors put on autographs of people they'd never met. Franzoni was not convinced. And sure enough as time passed, his calls to Williams were routinely ignored—"Ted never answers the telephone himself any more, so I have to wonder"—and his presence less and less sought after.

Janet Franzoni, Bob's wife, wrote me a letter complaining about how "Ted has changed." She said, "He seems so uncaring—witness Joe Lindia. . . . It's almost as though since he found he's bankable,

> *In his quixotic attempts to save his father from cheaters, John-Henry seemed forever and always after somebody, suing somebody, being sued by somebody. At one point, he even sued his own sister, Claudia.*

all he cares about is making money. . . . I liked him better when he was living in Islamorada and palling around with his fishing cronies." I spoke with Janet after Bob Franzoni died. She said Ted's treatment of him at the end "was one of the greatest disappointments of Bob's life."

How much of this was Ted's doing is, of course, impossible to say. The obvious would be to believe not much. He had *always* been bankable and had never worked at it more than enough to get what he needed and be gone. What had changed was how the benefits had spread to others. Loran Smith enlightened me on what John-Henry's methodology had come to in harvesting those benefits when describing a visit he had had with Ted in the late nineties. Loran is an old friend of mine, a fixture at the University of Georgia and a regular columnist for the *Athens Banner-Herald*. I had set up the visit; Ted wanted to see some pictures I had, and Loran volunteered to take them by. He was, as he put it, "always a sucker for a chance to chat with Ted Williams" (I'd introduced them years before). This time he had his wife, Myrna, along, a decided advantage since Ted Williams always had time for good-looking women.

John-Henry and his girlfriend were there at the Citrus Hills enclave, Loran said, "and Ted was talking with us and seemed to be enjoying himself, even though the strokes had obviously limited him, and when I said it was time for us to go, he said, 'No, it's time for lunch. You're staying.' We did, and it was great fun. And after lunch John-Henry and his girlfriend left. About an hour or so later when we were finally getting ready to leave, being *allowed* to leave, I asked Ted if he'd sign a copy of *My Turn at Bat*, which I'd brought along. And he did. And then Myrna asked if he'd mind signing a couple of autographs for our children. He said sure, and told one of his house staff to get him some paper."

Loran said Ted had the paper and was signing when the phone rang and the staffer called out that it was "for Mr. Smith." "I went and picked it up and John-Henry was on the other end. I don't know who contacted him or what was said, but he was very upset. He said, 'What's going on with those autographs?' I was shocked. He made it sound as if we were going to sell them. I explained what we'd asked for was for the family, nothing more, but that if it was an inconvenience we certainly didn't want to impose. He calmed down, but he still seemed upset. I don't think Ted even noticed what was happening. It was spooky."

I thought at the telling that none of this was consistent with the Ted Williams I had known. And with time and the numerous eruptions over Ted's autographs (and oft-challenged authenticity of same by John-Henry) that *weren't* so private, the headlines got tougher to take, especially for those who saw the damage being done to Ted's reputation. A man who had always given so much more than he had taken was now perceived as taking . . . taking . . . taking. In his quixotic attempts to save his father from cheaters, John-Henry seemed forever and always after somebody, suing somebody, *being* sued by somebody. At one point, he even sued his own sister, Claudia.

And then, almost mercifully, Ted Williams died. The claptrap was over, and the deserved eulogies and celebrations of his life could now begin. But just when it seemed safe to go back in the water, along came the outrageous, disgraceful aftermath, with John-Henry producing a will on a wrinkled, single sheet of oil-stained paper, purportedly signed by Ted to supersede an "official" will he had signed and had notarized in 1996. The first one had stipulated he be cremated and his ashes "spread off the coast of Florida where the water is very deep." This one, which Williams purportedly signed simply "Ted Williams" instead of the "Theodore S. Williams" that he customarily penned to official documents, said he wanted to be frozen, ostensibly in the hope of a future, dramatic resurrection.

Off his dead carcass went to the Alcor Life Extension Foundation in Scottsdale, followed closely by the contretemps: a whole new series of ugly headlines, except even bigger and blacker, with John-Henry paired off against Ted's first child, Bobby-Jo (Barbara Joyce) Ferrell and her husband Mark, who wanted Ted's body defrosted and returned to Florida for burial. The Ferrells were portrayed as trying desperately to defend Ted's dignity against such a bizarre ending, John-Henry as doing his damnedest to undermine it. Until the Ferrells ran out of money and had to agree to shut up to collect Bobby-Jo's inheritance, the battle waged on, serving as irresistible fodder for editorial cartoonists and late-night talk show humor. It was depressing, all the bile, all the scratching and clawing over "what Ted Williams really wanted."

But just when it seemed safe to go back in the water, along came the outrageous, disgraceful aftermath, with John-Henry producing a will on a wrinkled, single sheet of oil-stained paper.

I was spared the angst not only because I preferred to believe that the nurse at the hospital in Inverness was correct when she said Ted's spiritual priorities were in order before he passed on, but because I really didn't care what they did with his 83-year-old body. He wasn't in it anymore anyway. I wanted to be reassured that he hadn't bought in to such nonsense beforehand. My wife Donna reassured me.

She was watching one of the first of the televised reports of the cryonics controversy, and listened long enough to cluck her tongue and shake her head and say, "This is ridiculous. We *know* what he wanted. He told us."

"Told us what?" I said. "What are you talking about?"

"It's on the videotape. The video Josh and Caroline took when we were at Ted's place that last day."

I said I didn't understand. She said I must have been out of the room when it was taken. She got the tape and put it on and we watched the replay. It showed Ted, in a walker, giving Donna a kind of impromptu guided tour of the latest decorations and memorabilia in the house at Citrus Hills. At one point, Donna paused before an almost full-size picture of a beautiful dalmatian and said, "Oh, there's Slugger." Slugger was one of Ted's most prized possessions. They'd been buddies from the Keys and we'd gotten to know him there, and Ted always said how much the dog meant to him.

They had a "Ted Williams Day" at Fenway Park in Boston in the early nineties, and he signified his newly acknowledged love for the fans . . . by tipping his hat.

But, of course, Slugger was long gone. Ted said he'd had him cremated. And there on the video he said that's what he wanted, too, for himself. To be cremated, and his ashes combined with Slugger's. He said, "He and I are gonna be scattered together."

It was clear, lucid, unmistakable. If others want to believe that Ted Williams succumbed to a different persuasion at the end, they're free to do so. But we heard otherwise, and legal implications aside, that counts for me—at least as a way of establishing some dignity to the whole bloody mess. As Donna said, for Ted's sake.

I realize now I will never be able to think of Hernando, or Citrus Hills, or Inverness, or any of those places he frequented over the last years as being Ted Williams' home-on-earth. I think of that only as being Islamorada, where the greater (and less controversial) memories are stored; where for me it all began so long ago with an inauspicious hunt for tarpon with the best tarpon fisherman who ever lived. I know it's true that it's not the same there now. That the Keys aren't the same, that Islamorada isn't. Not that Ted Williams has been obscured. To the contrary. The street where Ted's house intersected (it was called Madero and List roads then, but you'd have been hard pressed to find the signs) is now "Ted Williams Way."

And the house that I came to admire has been upgraded two or three times since, going from functional and "comfortable" when Ted had it to downright pretentious. As I mentioned earlier, the last time I saw it advertised in a real estate journal, it was selling for more than two million dollars and was called "the Ted Williams estate" in the ads. Ted told me he'd paid less than $50,000 when he bought it, and thought it overpriced.

A number of his friends, and his first "favorite" guide, Jimmy Albright, who used to brag that Ted Williams sprang for a roof on his house when he (Jimmy) couldn't afford it, are gone. So is Jack Brothers. And the month before I wrote this, Manny & Isa's Restaurant closed. Manny, the cook, was a favorite of Ted's, supplying "the best Cuban sandwiches on the Keys," and Isa, his wife, bore the brunt of Ted's loud humor in the dining room. "You sure that's turtle steak, Isa?" Ted would say, trying to get a rise, turning heads. "Tastes like veal to me." They displayed on the front wall a framed page from my *SI* story on fishing with Ted, the portion highlighted that named the restaurant. But if they've closed down, they're still around, and I like to think they've put the picture back up somewhere. "Oh, that Ted," Isa said the last time we passed through and relieved her of one of her Key lime pies. "Oh, my, that Ted."

Much more is still intact, those things that provide such worthwhile memories. If the first great fishermen whose presence he sought (and who put up with his needling as he moved past them in expertise) are gone, others who knew him and fished with him are still around, and still talk about the zip he brought to their lives. George Hommell runs a worldwide fish and tackle business. George was the catalyst for Ted and me fishing in Costa Rica, and still talks about that trip (and still calls me "la Paloma," the Pigeon, for my failures at the poker table). When I called the other day, George fairly leaped into the retelling of an episode off the Exumas in the Bahamas when, in a 13-foot skiff, Ted caught "the biggest damn bonefish I've ever seen. When we tried to weigh it, it was too heavy for the scale." He said how proud he was that when Ted was invited to campaign for George Bush, the father, in New England during the 1988 presidential election, he had Hommell included in the party. "Me, a lowly fisherman."

Gary Ellis has equally warm memories. Ellis was Ted's primary guide "ten days a year for seven years" at the end. He remembers the fishing, sometimes including Bush, sometimes including Curt Gowdy, but more than that he remembers seeking Ted's input when he started the "Red Bone Celebrity Fishing Tournament" to raise money for cystic fibrosis research. Ellis' daughter, Nicole, had the disease. Ted not only lent his name, Ellis said, "he came down and lent his presence." Nicole, then four, sat on Ted's lap to talk, being careful, Ellis said, to "sit so that Ted could see her because a stroke had affected his vision. He talked with her like she was his best friend." Ellis said the tournament raised $16,000 that year,

"and we were ecstatic. But Ted kept lending his support, and since then we've raised almost a million dollars. And he never asked for anything. Not a thing. He was happy to do it. He *enjoyed* doing it."

I was thus reminded of the very last time Donna and I passed through Islamorada when Ted was still living there, on an occasion when two of

> *The announcer repeated for Ted to hear at last a verification of his childhood dream, "There goes the greatest hitter who ever lived!"*

Donna's best friends from Connecticut were in tow, Kathi Holt and Pam Foss. We were headed to Key West for recreation there, but since we'd be passing by, I called Ted to check his availability. He insisted we drop in.

Pam and Kathi easily qualified as Ted Williams' kind of women, almost prototypical: pretty, vivacious, and not at all disinclined to speak their minds. Except in Kathi's case, being too big a fan not to be enthralled, she was practically tongue-tied the whole time. ("I mean, what do you say to a legend?" she complained afterward, frustrated by her own restraint.) Pam made up for it. Much less familiar with Ted's credentials, she never stopped kidding him, and when we were getting ready to leave, blithely suggested he "autograph something" for her two boys.

Ted nodded and went upstairs to his bedroom, returning in short order with a large card inscribed to "Peter and Andrew, your pal, Ted Williams." Pam looked at it and sniffed. "How am I going to give them this, tear it in half?" she said. "Get back up there and get me two of these!" Ted gave her a hard look, broke into a grin, and padded back up the stairs. When he returned, still grinning, he had two cards signed. "Boy, it must be something, being married to you," he said to Pam out of the corner of his mouth.

I miss walking with him in strange, far-off places, marveling that he could move so fast with such a languid style, as though he had discovered an advanced form of ambling.

Before he died, there were a number of significant national acknowledgments of Ted Williams' achievements. He received, from George Bush, with whom he wound up fishing often in the Keys, America's highest civilian honor, the Presidential Medal of Freedom. They had a "Ted Williams Day" at Fenway Park in Boston in the early nineties, and he signified his newly acknowledged love for the fans (and even acknowledged the media) by tipping his hat. On New Year's Eve in 1999, he was named by, of all publications, the *Boston Globe* as New England's "top sports figure of the century." Dave Egan, "the Colonel" from criticisms long past, had once called him "the prize heel ever to wear the Boston uniform." I like to think that in whatever internment he wound up that Egan audibly will be flipping for the next millennium or two.

I wasn't there, but from all accounts, the most profoundly moving moment came at the 1999 All-Star Game at Fenway, when Williams threw out the first pitch on the 60th anniversary of his rookie year in Boston. He was 80 years old, no longer a splinter and no longer fully ambulatory. He circled the basepaths in a golf cart, and 40 other all-timers, baseball writers, and guests paid him tribute on national television. The announcer repeated for Ted to hear at last a verification of his childhood dream, "There goes the greatest hitter who ever lived!" (When I eventually asked him about it some time later, Ted said he was "equally proud" to have been inducted into the International Game Fishing Association Hall of Fame in 2000. And he said it like he meant it.)

But I think I understood the impact his presence made on others best of all on a winter's afternoon in Philadelphia, outside the press box at Veterans Stadium many years before. Until then I had only a very pedestrian sense of the influence his peers might have felt, my not being a fan, a rival, or a contemporary. I had generally regarded the homage paid as legitimate but probably more fan-made than historic, the Williams image aided and abetted by the media as just one more sports-page apotheosis of a "talent" in a game.

I was at the stadium for the Army-Navy game, on an especially cold December day. An academy intermediary said Joe DiMaggio was on hand and that we ought to meet. I said I didn't want to bother somebody for no good reason, but he insisted, and in the stairwell outside the press box, DiMaggio emerged. The friend gave him my name, which I was sure would mean absolutely nothing to him. And DiMaggio, in monotone, without expression, said, "Yes, I know you. You're the guy who wrote the Ted Williams book." That's all he said. That's all he needed to say. The *Ted Williams* book.

In the tenderness of memories, the hard edges fade. Now I confront, more often than I thought possible, the void that he has left in my life. I find myself, at quiet moments (and sometimes not so quiet, when something exciting passes my way that is reminiscent of past adventures), thinking about him, and remembering, and missing those things.

I miss fishing with him, and hunting with him, and talking with him. I miss walking with him in strange, far-off places, marveling that he could move so fast with such a languid gait, as though he had discovered an advanced form of ambling.

I miss playing comic, erratic tennis with him, and hearing him yelp with pleasure at winning a point. I miss arguing with him on subjects past and present, and enlightening him, and being enlightened *by* him. I miss his intuitive grasp of phoniness, and his consistent inability to hide a legitimate feeling.

I miss being told by him how smart I am—and being told otherwise when I have said or done something dumb. I miss kidding him, and being kidded by him. I miss hearing him say how lucky I am to be in his company, and how I should count my blessings. Yes, and I miss hearing his voice at the other end of the telephone line, coming to me from the side of his mouth, out of the blue. "It's only me."

I miss him.

Index